CLASSIC
Italian
RACING MOTORCYCLES

CLASSIC

Italian

RACING MOTORCYCLES

Mick Walker

OSPREY
AUTOMOTIVE

Page 1
*Libero Liberati, 1955 Italian Senior Championship
winner aboard the four-cylinder Gilera*

Page 2
*Walter Villa in full flight during one of his last rides
on the Harley-Davidson twin at the 1978 West
German GP held at the Nürburgring. By that time
the team was privately sponsored by the Nolan
helmet company*

Left
*Gandossi (5) and Chadwick (12), on Ducatis, lead
Provini (1) and Ubbiali (7) on their MV Agustas
during the 125 cc Ulster GP, August 1958*

Published in 1991 by Osprey Publishing
59 Grosvenor Street, London W1X 9DA

British Library Cataloguing in Publication Data

Walker, Mick
    Classic Italian racing motorcycles.
    1. Italy. Motorcycles. Racing
    I. Title
    796.75

ISBN 1-85532-182-3

Editor Ian Penberthy
Page Design Geoffrey Wadesley

Filmset and printed in Great Britain by
BAS Printers Limited, Over Wallop, Hampshire

Guzzi returned to the tarmac in 1969, when it captured a number of speed records on two and three wheels with tuned V7 roadsters. Here Giuseppe Dal Toé storms around the Monza banking

Contents

About the author

Mick Walker is an enthusiast for all forms of motor-cycle sport. He has been a successful competitor and has helped many to triumph with his profound knowledge of tuning. There is virtually no aspect of the business in which Mick has not been active at some point, and that includes being an importer of exotic Italian race-bred machines. Today, he heads a thriving company that specializes in the supply of spare parts to Ducati owners and racers around the world. He is also one of Osprey's most prolific authors.

Mick rode a variety of racers during the classic era, including an AJS 7R, Manx Norton, Greeves Silverstone, a brace of BSA Gold Stars, various Ducatis and even 50 and 125 cc Hondas.

Above

The author, on a Ducati 250 Mark 3 (10), nips inside the 750 Triumph Trident of Colin Dixon during the 1970 Thruxton 500-mile endurance race

Introduction

Above all else, Italy has a reputation for *style*, having gained fame for its beautiful architecture, up-to-the-minute fashion design, exotic cars, and motorcycles which display a rare combination of sheer style and exciting performance.

In the field of powered two-wheelers, the very first to be available in Italy were those manufactured by Hildebrand and Wolfmüller of Germany, which were sold by the Max Turkeiner organization of Milan around 1895. Another source in those early days were the great American marques, such as ACE, Harley-Davidson, Henderson and Indian.

The first pure-bred Italian motorcycles made their appearance at the beginning of the 20th century and included Bianchi, Borgo, Prinetti & Stucchi and Ferrera.

By the 1920s these companies had been joined, or replaced, by a number of newer concerns. Then came a period when the *pentarchia* (the famous 'big five' Italian bike builders), comprising Benelli, Bianchi, Garelli, Gilera and Guzzi, fought tooth and nail for a share of the market. This led to the creation of specialized racing departments within those factories, which produced a succession of exciting racers and record-breakers. They continued to do so right up to the outbreak of World War 2.

Until then, Italy's economy had been largely agri-

Italian Senior Championship, Rimini, March 1968: Benelli-mounted Renzo Pasolini leads Angelo Bergamonti (on a Morini) during the hotly-contested 250 cc race

cultural, but when the war ended in 1945, the country witnessed a rapid march towards industrialization and a boom in the sales of personal transport. Motorcycles were all the rage, and manufacturers responded by rushing headlong into support for road racing on an unprecedented scale.

This period—now referred to as the 'golden age of Italian motorcycling'—lasted until the mid 1950s, by which time the sales boom was coming to an end. Something had to give, and at the end of 1957 three of the largest and most successful teams—Mondial, Gilera and Guzzi—announced their retirement from the sport.

This improved the chances of such marques as MV Agusta, Bianchi, Benelli, Morini and Ducati, who continued to fly the red, white and green flag of Italy with considerable success until the Japanese sprang on to the world stage in the 1960s. Even so, MV Agusta continued to dominate the 'blue riband' 500 cc class until the mid 1970s.

Above
Mike Hailwood's 125 Paton, during the 1958 IoM TT. Left to right: Mike, Stan Hailwood, Vic Willoughby, Lino Tonti and Giuseppe Pattoni

Right
Geoff Duke riding the works Gilera 500 cc four in the Grand Prix of Nations, Monza, September 1956

In the lightweight categories, Italian machines provided world-class contenders—such as Morbidelli, Minerelli and Garelli—well into the 1980s, before finally being ousted by the all-powerful modern Japanese industrial machine.

Italy not only produced a host of world-beating machinery, but also a number of top riders. These included Carlo Ubbiali, Bruno Ruffo, Umberto Masetti, Tarquinio Provini, Walter Villa, Dario Ambrosini, Nello Pagani, Enrico Lorenzetti, Libero

Liberati, Paolo Pileri, Pier-Paolo Bianchi, Eugenio Lazzarini, Mario Lega and, most notably, Giacomo Agostini.

In the course of compiling this particular book, I was fortunate enough to come into contact with many people who were able to help in some way. Almost all gladly provided whatever assistance they could. Unfortunately, there were so many that there simply is not space available to list them all, but I shall be eternally grateful for the help I received.

I offer acknowledgement to the following, in no particular order of merit: John Surtees, Bill Lomas, John Kirkby, Doug Jackson, Barry Hickmott, Luigi Giacometti, Franco Valentini, Giorgio Grimandi, Gerolamo Bettoni, Arturo Magni, Gemma Pedretta, Hoss Elm, Herbert Namink, Jap de Jong, Tarquinio Provini, Arthur Wheeler and Michael Dregni.

Photographs came from a variety of sources, including Nick Nicholls, Len Thorpe, Phillip Tooth, George Nutall, Doug Jackson, Alan Kirk, Nadia Pavignani, Peter Richardson, Moto Guzzi, Moto Gilera, Ducati Meccanica, EMAP Archives, Peter Glover, Mark Wellings, Michael Dregni and Richard Walker; cover photography by Don Morley.

My thanks also go to Kim White, who made such an excellent job of typing the manuscript at short notice, and last, but not least, to the super-efficient Osprey editorial team, editor Ian Penberthy plus, of course, the guiding light of managing editor Nick Collins.

Classic Italian Racing Motorcycles is the fourth title in a series of books that look at the major players, around the world, who produced racing motorcycles during the 'classic' period. I sincerely hope that you glean as much enjoyment from reading the finished product as I have had in compiling it.

Mick Walker
Wisbech, Cambridgeshire

1

Aermacchi

Varese, a small provincial town near the Swiss border, has been a centre for the Italian aviation industry since 1912, when the firm of Nieuport-Macchi was established there by Giulio Macchi. In fact, many of the early aircraft were seaplanes, which accounted for the factory being sited on the shores of Lake Varese.

Nieuport-Macchi grew to quite a large size during World War 1, and continued—albeit under the fresh title of Aeronautica Macchi (soon abbreviated to Aermacchi)—to concentrate on aircraft in the years that followed.

The Varese company became one of the major participants in the famous Schneider Trophy series of seaplane races, and besides winning the event on

Bill Webster (seated) with the first 250 Aermacchi Ala d'Oro imported into Britain. The year is 1960, the venue Oulton Park

more than one occasion, also had the distinction of setting a new world speed record with the MC-72 seaplane in 1934. During World War 2, now concentrating upon land-based fighters, it produced some of Italy's finest warplanes to take part in the conflict.

Unable to resume its aviation activities after hostilities had ended, Aermacchi decided to begin production of a three-wheeled truck. This was followed by a decision to join the motorcycle boom which was sweeping Italy during the late 1940s. Company chiefs realized that to achieve their aims of producing an attractive, quality lightweight, they needed a top designer. Their choice was Ing. Lino Tonti, who had been at Benelli and had worked on aircraft engines during the war.

Tonti's first design for Aermacchi was a distinctly unorthodox 125 cc two-stroke, the engine pivoting in unit with the rear suspension. It sold in reasonable numbers and enjoyed some success in long-distance trials, such as the ISDT. Other designs followed, and in 1955 Ing. Tonti conceived a record-breaker, making full use of the wind tunnel and other resources belonging to the factory's aircraft division (which, by then, had resumed production of both military and civilian types).

Powered by double-overhead-cam engines of 48 and 74 cc, the Tonti-inspired streamliner was one of the very first examples of the 'Flying Cigar' machines, being very low and some 3.50 m (10 ft) in length. Positioned behind the rider, the engine was unusual in that it had its cylinder inclined *rearwards* at an angle of 20 degrees.

The overhead camshafts were driven by chain, while the bore and stroke dimensions were 44.5 × 43 mm for the larger unit, and 40 × 39 mm for

13

Superb Nick Nicholls action shot of Stuart Graham taking Bill Webster's 1961-type, long-stroke Ala d'Oro to sixth place in the 250 cc race at Silverstone, 7 April 1962. The photograph exudes speed and grace in every line

the smaller engine. With a compression ratio of 10:1, the maximum output was 9 bhp at 11,000 rpm for the 74 cc version, and 7 bhp at 12,000 rpm for the 48 cc unit—reasonable figures, considering the period and the forced reliance on low-grade fuel.

Other technical details included a four-speed gearbox, wet-sump lubrication, a space frame, 18 in. wheels and a dry weight of 97 kg (214 lb).

The record attempts were carried out on 4 April 1956, the venue being the Milano-Varese *autostrada*. Neither weather nor road conditions were particularly ideal, there being strong winds, but piloted by Massimo Pasolini (father of Renzo), the larger engine pushed the machine to a speed of 100.2 mph over the flying mile, and 108.8 mph over the flying kilometre. This broke, by a considerable margin, the records set only a few months previously by Germany's Adolf Baumm with his NSU 'hammock'.

With the smaller power unit, the standing mile was also broken at a speed of 51.25 mph.

Soon after the record spree, Ing. Tonti quit Aermacchi to join FB Mondial (see Chapter 7), and the company's directors chose the vastly experienced Ing. Alfredo Bianchi to succeed him. Previously with Alfa Romeo and Parilla, Bianchi had also manufactured his own Astoria engines and complete machines in the 1930s.

Ing. Bianchi's first task for his new employer was to design a brand-new production model from a sketch of an 'ideal machine', which had been penned by Count Mario Revelli. The latter was a well-respected car stylist, who had also been a racing motorcyclist and had won the 1925 500 cc Italian GP on a machine of his own manufacture.

The new design, the all-enclosed 175 Chimera, was introduced to the public on a wave of publicity at the Milan show in November 1956. Although billed by factory and press alike as the star of the show, the Chimera was destined never to sell in anything like the numbers hoped for, either in Italy or abroad.

Because of this, it was decided to 'undress' it and produce a more conventionally-styled 'naked' version. Ing. Bianchi was instructed to carry out a cosmetic facelift which, when completed, would transform the machine's appearance at the minimum of expense. Besides the restyling, the only other major alteration was to the rear suspension system, which was changed from the original, single horizontal suspension unit to the more conventional, vertical twin-shock layout.

Besides its futuristic bodywork, the Chimera also differed from acknowledged Italian motorcycle practice of the period by featuring a humble pushrod engine, rather than the more popular ohc type. This type of powerplant had been chosen not only because it was easier to maintain, but also because Ing. Bianchi believed that, even for a faster sports model, there was no need for an ohc design. He was to be vindicated on the latter point by the success of the racing version of the design which was to follow.

When first displayed at Milan in 1956, the Chimera had a capacity of 172.4 cc (60 × 61 mm), but before long a 246.2 cc (66 × 72 mm) version had also been made. Shortly after the new 'undressed' models began to appear (in both engine sizes), their sporting potential was being explored. In 1958 a tuned 175, giving 15.5 bhp instead of the standard model's 13 bhp (at the same 8000 rpm), was being campaigned in Italian sports machine races. A pukka racing version, the Ala d'Oro, was constructed in 1959. Producing some 20 bhp, it was good for a genuine 100 mph and became the main rival of the Morini Settebello in national, junior-category racing.

A 250 version appeared in the following year, making its début at Assen, the scene of the 1960

Engine from the first batch of 344 cc Aermacchi racers, circa 1964

Oulton Park action, 23 April 1962; Eric Cheers at speed on his race-modified 250 Ala Verde roadster, before the era of the modern two-stroke which transformed the quarter-litre class

180 mm Oldani twin-leading-shoe front brake and Ceriani forks from early 250/350 models

Dutch TT. Ridden by Alberto Pagani (son of the famous Nello), the pushrod Aermacchi came home a creditable ninth. If this result was not good enough, race experts were amazed when, against the cream of the latest works bikes, Pagani brought the Varese flat-single home in an outstanding fifth place a week later in the Belgian GP, held over the ultra-fast Spa Francorchamps course. Later that year, the bike was sent to Britain for evaluation and was raced to victory by Alan Shepherd at Scarborough.

Impressed with the prototype's display of speed and reliability, the management of Aermacchi—now owned jointly by the Italians and the American marque Harley-Davidson—decided to go ahead with a small batch of similar bikes for sale to private customers for the 1961 season. In addition, Pagani had been joined by Gilberto Milani as an official works development rider to contest the Italian Senior Championship and selected Grand Prix events.

The 1960 prototype had given 24 bhp at 8200 rpm, but a winter's development added two more horses, whilst maximum revs rose to 9000. As the engine was still of comparatively low power output for a racing 250, Ing. Bianchi paid special attention to weight-saving measures; the 1961 Aermacchi Ala d'Oro DS 250 over-the-counter racer tipped the scales at 102 kg (225 lb) in racing trim. Another important factor which helped offset the com-

paratively low power was that the long-stroke engine gave excellent torque from very low revs.

As on the standard production roadsters, the four-speed (closer-ratio) gearbox was gear driven from the engine and transmitted power through a wet, multi-plate clutch to the rear wheel. Equipped with a cast, three-ring piston with a compression ratio of 10:2:1, the engine featured a DS2 cam, 10 mm stellite tappets and a 30 mm Dell'Orto carburettor.

Except for a hotter DSS cam, an increase in maximum engine revolutions to 9200 and an extra 2 bhp, the 1962 Ala d'Oro was essentially unchanged. Unfortunately, the extra rpm precipitated a bout of mechanical disasters on the 1962 batch of engines, including broken connecting rods and shattered pistons. In an attempt to solve these shortcomings, the 1963 version was redesigned. The main changes were a forged piston, a shorter, stiffer con-rod (although the stroke remained unchanged at 72 mm), and an 'A' cam. These improvements also allowed the engine revs to be increased still further—up to 9400. Finally, with a tightening of the power-band, a five-speed gear cluster was specified.

A mini-redesign occurred in time for 1964, when the DS-S model was introduced. This sported revised short-stroke, 72 × 61 mm bore and stroke measurements, which gave a new capacity of 248.3 cc. With the engine now capable of 10,000 rpm, maximum power was boosted to 32 bhp at 9400 rpm.

Back in 1963 the first 350 Aermacchi racer had appeared, being basically an oversize 250. The first attempts at creating this machine could be traced back to March 1961, when Pagani had tested a prototype with a 293 cc (72 × 72 mm) engine. Originally, this capacity had been conceived for motocross events, not road racing.

A production version of the 293 cc engine was never built, instead Aermacchi went the whole hog, the result being a 344 cc (74 × 80 mm) version. In its first year of production (1963), only a handful were manufactured—all with four speeds. The first example made its début at Hockenheim in May 1963, ridden by Milani.

Serious production of the larger engine did not begin until 1964, by which time it sported five speeds, as did the quarter-litre bike.

These machines (and the 1965 versions) in both 250 and 350 form still retained wet clutches, stellite tappets and several features from the earlier engines. Although they handled beautifully, reliability became a problem once more, broken con-rods and valves being the major offenders.

It was evident to Aermacchi that either a major

redesign of the original concept was needed or, better still, something entirely new. The original idea was a double-overhead-camshaft version with several improvements to increase bottom-end reliability. In fact, two prototypes (both 250s) were built—the first privately by chief race mechanic Celestino Piva, and the second by Ing. Bianchi himself (having been suitably impressed with Piva's creation!) Sadly, Harley-Davidson put its foot down and insisted upon another pair of pushrod models.

The main improvements to both the 1966 model 250 and 350 pushrod racers were as follows: dry clutch, wider gears, larger-diameter crankshaft flywheels, improved piston, connecting rod and big-end bearing and larger carburettor (35 mm for the 250 and 38 mm for the 350). Maximum rpm of the 250 was 9800, and of the 350, 8000.

For 1967 more modifications were introduced, such as a small-diameter outside flywheel, internal flywheels that were no longer full flywheels but bobweights, 10 mm chrome tappets (upgraded later to 12 mm to give greater reliability), a different timing cover, and modified crankcases with two ball-race main bearings on the nearside and the nearside crankcase increased in length to accommodate the extra bearing. Some 250s, and the majority of works

Pilot's eye view of 1964 Ala d'Oro. The layout was the same for both 250 and 350 cc versions

The Varese factory produced this dohc prototype in 1965, but it was never put into production

Aermacchi 250 motor on display at the Earls Court show, September 1967. By then, it sported five speeds and a dry clutch, plus stronger internals

engines, had special eccentric rockers; this also applied to short-stroke 350, 382 and 402 engines, which appeared later.

The year 1968 saw more changes, a works short-stroke special making an appearance for the 350 cc class. This displaced 349.2 cc (77 × 75 mm) and featured a forged 11:5:1 piston, N6 cam, 12 mm tappets, and a 38 mm carburettor. It produced 42 bhp at 8400 rpm and was good for around 135 mph on optimum gearing. Kel Carruthers rode just such a machine to third spot in the 1968 World Championship behind Giacomo Agostini, on an MV three, and former Aermacchi works rider Renzo Pasolini with a Benelli four.

In 1969 Milani, Carruthers and the young Irish star Brian Steenson gained a trio of second places in the Yugoslavian GP, Spanish GP and Isle of Man TT respectively.

British rider Alan Barnett, on importer Syd Lawton's machine, came second in the 1970 Junior TT in the Isle of Man, averaging 98.16 mph, after lapping at 99.32 mph—an outstanding performance. Another rider who campaigned the Varese singles with great success during this period was Angelo Bergamonti, who later signed to ride for MV Agusta.

There were also a number of attempts to create a viable 500 cc class machine. These included capacities of 382 cc (78 × 80 mm), 387 cc (78.5 × 80 mm) and finally, in 1969, 402 cc (80 × 80 mm). All valiant efforts, but swept aside by the oncoming tide of two-strokes as the new decade dawned. Before looking at Aermacchi's own attempts in this sector, it is worth taking a detailed look at the machine which promised so much but, in reality, delivered so little—the Linto.

In basic terms, the Linto was a pair of 250 Ala d'Oro cylinders and heads coupled together on a common crankcase. Designed by Ing. Lino Tonti (aided by fellow engineer Alcide Boitti) as a private venture, with financial backing from motorcycle enthusiast Umberto Premoli, the Linto made its competition début at Rimini at the beginning of April 1968. Two works prototypes were ridden by Pagani and Guiseppe Mandolini, and although electrical

Left

The crankshaft from a 1968 production 350 cc Ala d'Oro. Note the three-ring forged piston and crankpin end plugs

Below left

The cylinder barrel from the 1968 production 350 cc Ala d'Oro

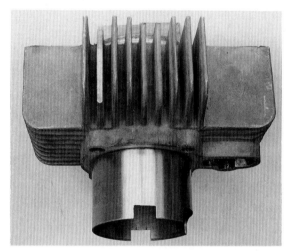

troubles stopped both machines, they showed considerable potential.

The Linto's engine consisted of the 1968-type 248.3 cc (72 × 61 mm) Aermacchi top ends (barrels, cylinder heads, valve gear, cams, pistons and conrods), but the four-bearing crankshaft was, like the crankcase, a one-off. The cranks were set at 360 degrees, instead of 180 degrees as on the original bench-test engine. This was an attempt to cure the excessive vibration which plagued the original. The gear primary drive was taken from the centre of the crankshaft, via a countershaft, to the dry clutch and six-speed gearbox.

After a season of further development, a batch of 15 Lintos were built for the 1969 season. Two of these were earmarked for Pagani and Jack Findlay, who had come second in the 1968 500 cc World

Below

Swiss engineer/rider Marly Drixl created an interesting 350 Drixton-Aermacchi

Above
Works rider Angelo Bergamonti at the foot of Bray Hill during the 1969 250 cc IoM TT. He retired from the race when his machine developed a serious oil leak

Left
Syd Lawton had taken over as British importer after Bill Webster's untimely death in 1963. He is seen here at the 1969 IoM TT with the first 382 cc Aermacchi engine to reach the UK. It is mounted in a Rickman Metisse chassis

Overleaf
Barnett during his historic second-place ride in the 1970 Junior TT at Ramsey

Championship on his McIntyre-Matchless. Besides these 'works' machines, the other 13 were sold, at £1300 each, to leading privateers, including Swiss-Hungarian Gyula Marsovszky, Australian Johnny Dodds, West German Walter Scheimann and Britain's Lewis Young.

Work on the prototype engines had raised the power output from 61 to 64 bhp at 10,000 rpm. The compression ratio was 10:1 and carburation by a pair of 35 mm instruments, whilst the frame had been modified during the development period and was both neater and sturdier. Suspension was by Ceriani, and the stopping power was provided by Fontana—

Englishman Alan Barnett lapped the Isle of Man circuit at 99.32 mph, during the 1970 Junior TT, on Syd Lawton's Aermacchi—an outstanding achievement

Above

A new breed—with the writing clearly on the wall for the ageing, flat-single four-strokes, the Varese factory came up with a twin-cylinder aircooled 'stroker' to challenge the Japanese

Above left

The twin-cylinder Linto engine designed by Ing. Lino Tonti. Essentially a pair of 250 Aermacchi top ends on a common crankcase, it promised much, but delivered little

Left

Aermacchi's first racing 'stroker' was this 123.1 cc (56 × 50 mm) piston-port single. Australian star Kel Carruthers is shown here during the 1969 TT, in which he finished second at an average speed of 84.43 mph

both brakes featured twin leading shoes, the front one being a double-sided 220 mm device.

With a weight of 135 kg (297 lb)—the same as the much less powerful Matchless G50 single—the Linto seemed to have great potential. This was particularly so after some good results achieved by Pagani during 1968, including a second behind Agostini (MV) in the East German GP.

Although Pagani went on to win the 1969 Italian GP at Imola, the production version proved a terrible disappointment for all concerned. Soon there was a host of Lintos with 'For Sale' signs on them in the race paddocks of the Continental circus.

Pagani continued to race the works Linto until mid 1971, before switching to MV, but the problems were never really solved, even though several changes were made, including a switch to Dansi electronic ignition for the 1970 season. That Imola victory was to remain the model's only classic win. In the end, it was the rise of the big two-strokes, such as the Kawasaki three and Suzuki twin, which finally signalled the end of the road for Tonti's creation.

As for Aermacchi itself, it had begun a new era when, in 1967, the Varese company had built its first two-stroke racer. This had been derived by Peter Durr from the existing 123.15 cc (56 × 50 mm) roadster. The West German tuning wizard had succeeded in doubling the power of the touring model, taking it from 10 bhp at 6750 rpm to 20 bhp at 9200 rpm. In fact, in the prototype, most of the engine parts were the same, including the crankshaft and its bearings, which withstood failure after several gruelling tests.

After many laps of Monza, in June 1967, the prototype of the simple, single-cylinder, piston-ported 'stroker' made its racing début in the following month at the new Zingonia circuit, near Bergamo, in the first Italian Senior Championship event of the year. After a slow start, Pagani's machine (still with the roadster's four speeds) made its way quickly through the field to finish a very promising third, behind the Mondial and the Montesa of the Villa brothers (which both sported rotary disc induction and eight speeds!).

Encouraged by this success, Aermacchi decided to build some production versions for sale to private customers. To this end, experiments were soon being carried out with different gearboxes—a conventional five-speed, close-ratio cluster, and an interesting 'overdrive' system (like that of the Kreidler 50 cc

Start of the 1975 250 cc Belgian Grand Prix, Harley-Davidson (Aermacchi) riders Rougerie (14) and Villa (2) scream their twins into action. They finished second and third respectively

GP bike of the early 1960s) with eight ratios, four controlled by a pedal and four by a twistgrip. Later still, a *ten-speed* type was also tested. However, production examples all came with conventional five-speed boxes. Two other changes were a switch from helical to straight-cut primary drive gears and modified porting.

The engine, slung below the frame's single top tube, breathed through a 27 mm Dell'Orto carburettor. Ignition was by a Dansi flywheel magneto and external HT coil, the points and condenser being mounted on the magneto's stator plate.

All this added up to an extremely lightweight motorcycle, which tipped the scales at only 80 kg (176 lb).

The definitive version appeared at the beginning of 1969. It featured a new, much more attractive, double-cradle frame, new cylinder head and barrel, new piston and other more minor alterations. Power output had been increased to 24 bhp—high for what was, after all, only a piston-port type.

Above
The new twin was first tested at Modena on 25 February 1971. The rider is Renzo Pasolini

Riders such as Kel Carruthers, Johnny Dodds and Silvano Berterelli all scored World Championship points that year, the highlight being Carruthers' runner-up spot in the Isle of Man. Even better was to follow in 1970, with Dodds winning the opening round at the Nürburgring, and Angelo Bergamonti coming home third in Yugoslavia.

That year had also seen the appearance of an interesting special built around the little Aermacchi 'stroker'. Constructed for the Mainini brothers, well-known dealers in Milan, by frame specialist Marly Drixl, it was even lighter in weight at 74 kg (163 lb). The engine had also received attention, being converted to disc-valve induction and employing a larger 32 mm carburettor.

The lessons learnt by Aermacchi with the 125 cc single helped with the creation of the next new racing machine from the Varese plant. First mooted in 1969, it followed the successful Yamaha TD/TR racing design, which Aermacchi's Stateside partner was keen to counter in American events. Therefore, the new bikes were to be 250 and 350 cc twins with orthodox, aircooled, two-stroke power units without disc valves.

Unfortunately, pressure of other work in the experimental department at Varese was to delay development of the twins, the result being that it was not until March 1971 that the design was first track tested (in 250 cc form). This took place at Modena in the hands of former Benelli ace Renzo Pasolini, who later that week raced the same machine at the same circuit.

Despite crashing half-way through the event, Pasolini took seventh place against an international all-star line-up, including the likes of World Champions Phil Read and Dave Simmonds.

Chief designer William Soncini stated that he was 'very well pleased' with the initial results of testing and racing—as well he might have been, since the engine's 46 bhp (at 10,500 rpm) was over 11 bhp up on the best figures ever achieved with the horizontal 250 pushrod single. Furthermore, the new twin's weight matched the single's 113 kg (250 lb) once the prototype's heavy iron cylinders were replaced by chrome-bore, light-alloy components, which produced a saving of 11 kg (24 lb).

The Varese factory offered over-the-counter 250 and 350 versions of its works two-stroke twins. This is a 1974 RR 250 with watercooling, dual Scarab discs at the front and a Fontana rear brake. High prices limited sales against the Yamaha TZ series

Lubricated by a 20:1 petroil mixture, the twin had the same bore and stroke dimensions as the 125 single, giving a capacity of 246.3 cc. Carburettors were 30 mm Dell'Ortos, and the Dansi electronic ignition had the under-seat coils fed by a spark-generating coil and pick-up on the nearside end of the crankshaft.

Many design features were aimed at simplifying maintenance and bypassing the need for specialized workshop equipment. For example, the two crankshaft assemblies were coupled by a split sleeve and two cotter pins, and could be separated with nothing more elaborate than a spanner. Bottom-end work was further assisted by the horizontal splitting of the crankcase. Moreover, although the primary drive was by straight-cut gears, the six-speed, close-ratio gearbox was bolted to the crankcase so that either unit could be removed independently.

By the time the 1972 season came around, a 347.4 cc (64 × 54 mm) version had joined the original quarter-litre model. In addition, Japanese Mikuni carburettors were specified.

Works rider Pasolini contested both classes of the World Championship on the twins which, at that stage, were still aircooled. He was particularly suc-

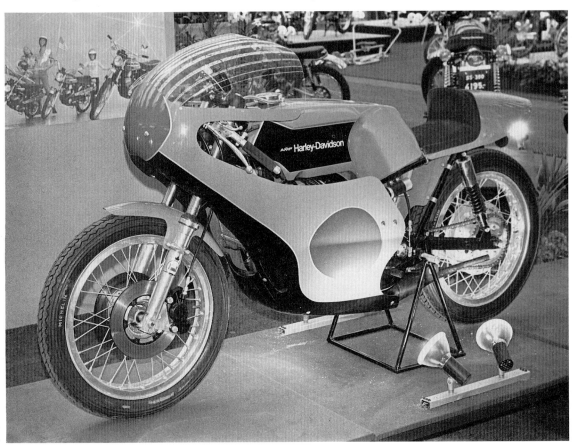

cessful in the smaller class, and after winning three rounds (Italy, Yugoslavia and Spain), he lost the title to Yamaha's Jarno Saarinen by a single point. Furthermore, although he failed to win a GP on the 350, Pasolini still managed to finish third in the points table, thanks to regular leader-board places throughout the year.

Great things were expected from the combination of Pasolini and Aermacchi in 1973. However, after débuting a watercooled 350 at the Italian GP and, in the process, breaking the 200 kph lap barrier for the first time on a machine of this capacity at Monza, Pasolini was to lose his life in a horrific crash in the very next race. It occurred as he was battling for the lead in the 250 cc Grand Prix and also claimed the life of Saarinen.

The crash effectively stopped the Aermacchi challenge in its tracks, although a number of riders, including the Frenchman Michel Rougerie and Gianfranco Bonera, had occasional rides on the machines later that year. It also halted development of a 500 cc twin (66.7 × 70 mm) which Pasolini had been testing.

In 1974—with AMF Harley-Davidson on the tank (Aermacchi had sold its remaining shares and returned solely to the aviation business)—the Varese two-stroke twins were back with a vengeance. With Bonera having departed to MV Agusta, the new team

Interesting, but unsuccessful, four-carb 500 cc H-D twin, circa 1975. Note brake disc below carburettor, rather than on rear hub

Four-carb 500 cc twin, February 1975. The engine was later mounted in a Bimota chassis and raced by Vanes Francini in the Italian Senior Championship

leader was the experienced Walter Villa, who was backed up by Rougerie.

The latest version of the 250 (now also water-cooled) pumped out an impressive 54 bhp, something even Yamaha could not match that year. The result was the factory's first ever World Championship title.

The following year Villa and Rougerie repeated their winning performance. Villa came in first with Rougerie runner-up in the title stakes. Despite a horde of bikes, Yamaha still could not offer an effective challenge.

The Varese team also chose to bring out a development of the 1973 500 twin (but now watercooled) for the 1975 season. However, although fast, this four-carburettor, 90 bhp device was never the success it was hoped to be, and the engine was later

Right
Walter Villa became the 1976 250 and 350 cc World Champion on the Varese two-stroke twins. Earlier, he had taken the 1974 and 1975 250 cc titles

Below
Villa on his way to victory in the 1976 250 cc Finnish GP at Imatra

Technical details of Villa's 1976 250 H-D, which developed 58 bhp at 12,000 rpm. The specification included watercooling, six speeds, Campagnolo enclosed disc front brake and magnesium wheels

made available to Bimota for a private effort (with Bimota chassis), which was raced in 1976 by Vanes Francini.

In 1976 Bonera returned to the Varese camp after two seasons with MV. Together with Villa, he rode the unbeatable 250, plus the, by now, highly-competitive 350. The result was the best ever in the company's history, Villa becoming a double World Champion by taking both the 250 and 350 cc titles to make it four world crowns in three years!

The 1976 250 bikes gave 58 bhp at 12,000 rpm, while the 350s produced 70 bhp at 11,400 rpm. This

resulted in maximum speeds of approximately 155 and 165 mph respectively.

If 1976 had been one of glory, 1977 was the reverse. Plagued by financial problems, the Varese plant could no longer afford to run a proper Grand Prix team, and Villa was forced to defend his titles with a privately-organized team backed by Nolan Helmets. The result was inevitable, performances becoming worse as the season progressed. Even so, Villa's new team-mate, Franco Uncini, still managed to finish second in the 250 cc class, while Villa came third. The 350, however, was completely out of the frame.

By the following June (1978), the Varese factory was declared bankrupt and, subsequently, was sold to a local company by the name of Cagiva . . . the rest is modern history.

2
Benelli

Six *fratelli* (brothers), all young enough to accept advice from an intelligent and loving mother, created a tiny mechanical workshop in the Adriatic coastal town of Pesaro; the year was 1911. From this humblest of beginnings was to spring one of the most famous marques in Italian motorcycle racing history.

Initially, the workshop's activities were restricted to the repair of automobiles and motorcycles, and anything else mechanical, even guns. Soon, however, the Benelli brothers began to carry out limited manufacturing on their own account. They started producing components for cars and aircraft, a process which accelerated with the outbreak of World War 1 in 1914.

At the end of hostilities, in 1918, the brothers turned their engineering skills to a new field. In Italy, and throughout Europe, there was a rapidly-growing requirement for cheap mechanical transport—a demand which gave rise not only to a number of ultra-lightweight motorcycles, but to various bicycle attachments (such as the Wall Auto Wheel in Britain). Thus, the Benellis designed and built their first engine, a 98 cc two-stroke unit, which was mounted in front of the steering column of an orthodox bicycle (á la Velosolex). Drive from this auxiliary engine was taken, by chain, to the

One of the pre-war double-knocker 250 cc Benelli singles being raced by Luigi Ciai at the Circuito delle Terme di Caracalla, *summer 1945*

front wheel. All very well, except for one tiny problem—the Benelli engine produced *too much* power for the hapless cycle.

There was only one solution to the dilemma: design a frame which could cope with the power and, thus, the first real Benelli motorcycle was conceived.

Introduced in 1921, the new Benelli sported a conventional frame and girder forks. The engine employed magneto ignition and transmitted its power via a separate, two-speed gearbox and thence chain to the rear wheel.

At this point, only five of the Benelli brothers were involved in the workshop enterprise—the sixth, Francesco, had become a Lancia car agent in Ancona. Of the others, Giovanni and Giuseppe were the technical wizards, while Domenico and Filippo kept the wheels of industry turning with their flair for administration—in other words, they were gifted 'pen-pushers'. This left Antonio (known to everyone as Tonino), who was the youngest of the six and had a burning desire to prove his worth as a road racer.

By 1923, after a 125 cc model had been launched, Tonino finally got his chance, and no less an event than the Italian Grand Prix at Monza was chosen for the début. Displaying a mixture of youthful exuberance and potential greatness, he took his machine (bored out to 147 cc) to an impressive fifth place in the hotly-contested 175 cc class.

The following year saw Tonino Benelli score his

Works 250 Benelli, as raced by Dario Ambrosini in 1950 when he became World Champion

first victory, in the Parma-Poggio di Bereto hill-climb, one of the major events on the Italian sporting calendar at the time. There were more successes in 1925 and 1926, but the year 1927 was to establish Tonino as a major star.

In this, he was helped by the new 175 cc four-stroke sports model, which was specially prepared by Giovanni Benelli. By the end of that year, Tonino had won countless races, including both Italian classics—the Lario (known as the Italian TT) and the Grand Prix at Monza. He also took the 175 cc National Championship and set several new world speed records for various distances.

The machine with which Tonino scored these successes was powered by an sohc 172 cc (62 × 57 mm) engine, and its extremely light weight of only 86 kg (190 lb) made the very best use of the engine's 10 bhp at 6500 rpm, giving a maximum speed in excess of 80 mph. This was a truly fabulous performance for its time, resulting in rival riders and their machinery simply being outpaced.

Other factories strove to close the gap, but before they could do so, brothers Giovanni and Giuseppe furnished Tonino with an even more potent piece of machinery in the shape of a double-knocker version. This featured 'square' 60.5 mm bore and stroke dimensions, which upped the capacity slightly to 173.8 cc. From this was developed a 248.8 cc

(65 × 75 mm) model, which made its début in 1935 and, in modified form, was raced by the Pesaro factory until as late as the 1961 season.

Lone hand Tonino was joined by several other riders, among them Baschieri—who gained Benelli's first major foreign victory when he won his class in the 1931 Swiss GP—Aldrghetti, Alberti and the great Dorino Serafina, who was destined to sweep Gilera to success a few years later. In 1933 Alberti won the 175 cc class at the Dutch TT, and in the following year, the factory's first foreign jockey, the Dutchman Goor, cleaned up in the Belgian and French meetings. Successful attempts were also made at establishing new world distance records but, at that stage, Benelli fought shy of the ultimate challenge, the Isle of Man.

An accident caused Tonino Benelli's retirement from the sport and brought a curtailment of the Pesaro company's racing activities during the period 1935–6. By then, the marque had grown to be one of the *pentarchia* (the famous 'big five' Italian bike builders), the others being Bianchi, Garelli, Gilera and Guzzi.

Thus, the new 250 did not achieve its first success until 1937, when Martelli won the Milano-Taranto marathon. By the following season, the quarter-litre model had arrived in style, winning victory wherever it competed, with riders such as Lorenzetti (later to achieve fame as a Guzzi man in the 1940s and 1950s), Francisci and Rossetti.

Revised dohc Benelli single with telescopic front forks and swinging-arm rear suspension, spring 1951

The great Dario Ambrosini, tragically killed during a crash while practising for the French GP at Albi, July 1951. Following his death, Benelli withdrew from full-scale support for several years

Leo Tartarini (later to become head of Italjet) in Bologna during his winning ride on a 125 cc Benelli, Giro d'Italia (Tour of Italy) 1953

Then came the achievement which made Benelli an internationally-famous name, the 1939 Lightweight TT. Irishman Ted Mellors, riding the sole Benelli in the race, won the event against an array of works machines, which included supercharged DKWs and Guzzis.

To counter the ever-increasing challenge of the 'blowers', Benelli accepted that it needed its own superchargers, attacking the problem from two different angles. The first was simply to equip one of the existing dohc singles with a compressor, but the other was a far more interesting project. Displayed on the company's stand at the 1939 Milan show, it was a watercooled, 249.4 cc (42 × 45 mm), four-cylinder model. Benelli claimed 52 bhp at 10,000 rpm and a maximum speed of 143 mph without streamlining! Unfortunately, neither of these projects was to be raced before the war came along, and with it the almost total destruction of Benelli's production facilities.

As if this was not bad enough, all the machinery, which the brothers had saved from the ruins of their factory, was packed off to the Fatherland by the Germans, and with it went everything else that might possibly have been of use, if only for scrap. Thankfully, the precious racing bikes escaped. They were

dismantled and concealed, the watercooled four being hidden for the duration of hostilities in a dried-up well!

Resumption of activity was extremely difficult after the war, since it entailed starting from scratch all over again. There was also a split in the family, when Giuseppe, together with his sons Marco and Luigi, left to form the rival Motobi enterprise. This did not affect the racing side quite so much, as even in the summer of 1945, the pre-war singles had been brought out of hiding and revived to fight Moto Guzzi yet again on tracks throughout Italy.

Ciai, Francisci and Martelli were the men who donned leathers to give Benelli victories during the period 1945–7. Then, in 1948, Dario Ambrosini rejoined Benelli, after a spell as a Guzzi rider, and immediately brought international success. Victories in the Swiss and Italian GPs, and the Lightweight TT in the Isle of Man, culminated in this gifted rider winning the 250 cc World Championship during 1950.

In 1951, after winning the Swiss Grand Prix at a soaking Bremgarten circuit in Berne and finishing second—only seconds behind winner Tommy Wood (Guzzi)—in the TT, Ambrosini was killed when his mount skidded on molten tar whilst practising for the French round at Albi. This tragedy hit the Benelli family hard and resulted in their virtual withdrawal from racing.

Not until 1959 did they feel inclined to pick up

the threads again. That year Benelli came back with a strong effort consisting of a considerably revised double-knocker 250 single and a trio of top riders (Dickie Dale, Geoff Duke and a promising young Italian, Silvio Grassetti).

The pre-war, and early post-war, Benellis had long-stroke 65 × 75 mm engines, giving a capacity of 248.8 cc and a power output of 25 bhp at 8000 rpm when Mellors won the 1939 TT; power was increased to 27 bhp at 8700 rpm by 1948. In 1951 the bore and stroke dimensions were changed to square 68 × 68 mm measurements, long favoured by rivals Guzzi, and the power boosted to 29 bhp at 9400 rpm.

For its comeback in 1959, chief engineer Ing. Savelli carried out a number of changes, including a short-stroke 248.1 cc (70 × 64.8 mm) engine with a totally redesigned appearance to provide neater, more modern lines. These changes also resulted in the power output being raised to 33 bhp at 11,500 rpm, while a six-speed gearbox was added. The running gear was also updated with new telescopic forks, a duplex chassis with swinging-arm rear suspension, full-width alloy brake hubs and an alloy dolphin fairing. Tests were carried out on a desmodromic version, too. One of the revised Benelli's few successes that year came in the non-championship Swiss GP at Locarno where, on a tight, twisting circuit, Geoff Duke scored one of his last victories before retiring at the end of the season.

It was soon realized that the single, even in revamped form, could scarcely be expected to hold its own against the latest machines which, by 1960, included the MV and Ducati twins, to say nothing of the new four-cylinder Japanese Honda. So, in

The 1959 season saw Benelli return to big-time racing with an improved and updated dohc single. It was designed by Ing. Savelli, who is seen here with rider Dickie Dale (left)

Above
Dale in action, on one of the revamped 250 singles, during a test session at Monza on 7 April 1959

Right
Experimental castings for a desmodromic version of the 250 single-cylinder engine, 1959

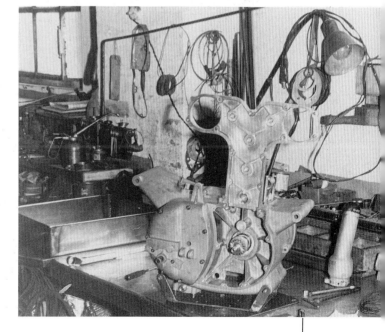

June that year, Benelli produced another four of its own, this time an up-to-the-minute aircooled model. Completely unexpected, it created headlines around the world when it was announced.

Like its predecessor, the new engine followed the, by now, classic engineering layout. Its four cylinders were set transversely across the frame, there were double overhead camshafts with a central gear drive, and a geared primary drive, between the first and second pots, on the nearside, to reduce overall width.

The only distinctive characteristic feature of the

Above
*In early 1962 British racing entrant Fron Purslow
acquired one of the works 250 Benelli singles.
Subsequently, it was raced with a fair amount of
success by Mike Hailwood and, later, Ralph Bryans*

Left
*Works rider Silvio Grassetti in action, on one of the
Benelli singles, at a very wet Cesenatico, April 1960*

Benelli design were the vertical cylinders; MV, Gilera and Honda favoured inclined units. At first, cast-iron cylinders were fitted, but later these were changed for light-alloy components with austenitic liners.

The bore and stroke dimensions were 44 × 40.5 mm, giving a capacity of 246.32 cc, while the compression ratio was 10:5:1 originally, but was later upped to 11:1. The power output was *claimed* to be 40 bhp at 13,000 rpm. Ignition was initially by battery coil, but this was soon changed to a Lucas magneto with a short bevel-gear drive from a central gearwheel on the crankshaft. The magneto was located in the centre of the crankcase at the front. A multi-plate dry clutch was employed on the nearside of the unit-construction engine/gearbox assembly, which had six speeds.

There was also considerable experimentation with the lubrication system. At first, the oil tank was mounted on the nearside of the machine. Then it was shifted in front of the fuel tank. Finally, Benelli engineers, headed by Ing. Savelli, decided to place the oil tank under the crankcase, thus not only obtaining better cooling, but also lowering the centre of gravity.

Other important modifications were carried out to the cylinder head, the crankshaft and to the inlet and exhaust ports. The weight of the first prototype was 120 kg (264 lb), but this was reduced by over 11 kg (25 lb) prior to the machine's first race at the beginning of the 1962 season. In the main, this was due to the use of revised brakes (from the 1959 Benelli single type to Oldani units), deletion of the frame-mounted oil tank and, most importantly, a lighter twin-cradle frame.

Its race début came at the international Imola Gold Cup races in April 1962, when Grassetti challenged Tarquinio Provini, who rode a works Morini single, before retiring when a valve touched a piston. At

Cesenatico, the new Benelli was really flying, beating the Honda fours of Tom Phillis and Jim Redman.

Only a week later, in the Spanish GP at Barcelona's twisting Montjuich Park circuit, it menaced the Honda team again, Grassetti really pressing Bob McIntyre, before retiring with ignition trouble. Later that year, at San Remo, another extremely tortuous circuit, Grassetti challenged the Provini–Morini combination once more, until a lurid slide halted his bid. However, the Benelli four did not get as far as the start-line for the all-important Italian GP at Monza. During practice for the event, one of the magneto drive gears broke beyond repair.

Development continued throughout 1963, accelerating once Tarquinio Provini left Morini to join Benelli at the end of that year. It is worth recalling that before he actually signed, Provini took his prospective mount for a 100-mile spin on the *public highway* before saying, 'Yes, I'll race it'. Amazing when you realize that the machine was in full racing trim, complete with open pipes and streamlining! Upon his return, he clinched the deal by shaking hands with Giovanni Benelli at the Pesaro factory.

Grassetti with the original prototype aircooled Benelli 250 four-cylinder model, spring 1960. The press boys have their notepads at the ready

The 1964 250 four was some 16 kg (35 lb) lighter and had seven instead of six gears, but even so— much to the chagrin of Provini—his replacement in the Morini team, Giacomo Agostini, beat the 31-year-old maestro to the Senior Italian Championship title. The dual between the two riders made it the most hotly-contested Italian Championship race for many a long year.

For 1965 the four was improved further, with changes to the crankshaft, heads and gearbox. Power output was now 52 bhp at 16,000 rpm. Experiments were also conducted on the braking system at Modena in March. Hydraulically-operated, twin disc brakes were fitted to the front wheel in place of the 220 mm Oldani drum previously employed. Provini was quoted as saying: 'The discs are much lighter and more efficient.' By May Benelli had taken this a stage further and had fitted a disc unit to the rear wheel. The brakes were not Italian, but American, being manufactured by Bo Gehring of Moto TEC, Harper's Ferry, West Virginia.

The magneto had also been changed to one of American origin—from an outboard four-cylinder two-stroke engine—which replaced the original Lucas unit. Experiments were being carried out with transistorized ignition, too.

The frame had been lowered and shortened, while

Above
A close-up of the prototype engine. It would be two years before it was raced in anger

Right
The four-cylinder power unit as it appeared in spring 1962. It had been revised considerably since its first appearance, there being notable changes to the lubrication and ignition systems

the offside tube of the cradle was made so that it could be removed to assist engine dismantling.

These changes, together with Agostini's departure from Morini to MV Agusta, were instrumental in Provini winning the 1965 and 1966 Italian Senior Championship titles. However, perhaps the most outstanding performance of Provini and the Benelli four came in the 1965 Italian GP. Riding superbly in drizzling rain, and urged on by a near hysterical crowd, Provini left Phil Read—out for the first time on the four-cylinder Yamaha—and teammate Mike Duff far behind as he lapped the entire field to win at an average speed of 94.52 mph.

The same meeting also saw Provini out for the first time on an experimental, overbored, 322 cc

(50 × 40.6 mm), four-cylinder Benelli, and despite
two pit-stops to change plugs, he snatched third
place ahead of Frantisek Stastny (Jawa). Benelli
claimed 53 bhp at 14,000 rpm, and said that the main
advantage was increased low-down torque and
improved acceleration. From this was developed a
343.19 cc (51 × 42 mm) version—with four valves
per cylinder.

Sadly, a serious crash, during practice for the 1966
Isle of Man TT, ended Provini's racing career. The
man chosen to replace the old master was the bespec-
tacled Renzo Pasolini.

Right from the start of the 1967 season, 'Paso'
began to make the sparks fly, prompting headlines
such as the one which appeared on the front page
of *Motor Cycle News* dated 22 March 1967: 'New 500
Benelli wins Modena!' The story went on to say that
Renzo Pasolini had given the new 491 cc four victory
in its first race, at the Modena circuit, near Bologna,
on the previous Sunday. Reputed to develop 82 bhp
at 11,000 rpm, the 16-valve motor, however, was
'not quite so fast as the 500 MV-three ridden by
World Champion Giacomo Agostini'. After losing

Right
*Provini in vivid action on the Benelli 250 four,
summer 1964. Even his riding skill, however, could
not transform it into a serious challenger that year*

Below
*Benelli 250 four, as used by Grassetti during practice
for the Italian Grand Prix at Monza, September 1962.
A broken magneto bevel-drive shaft kept it out*

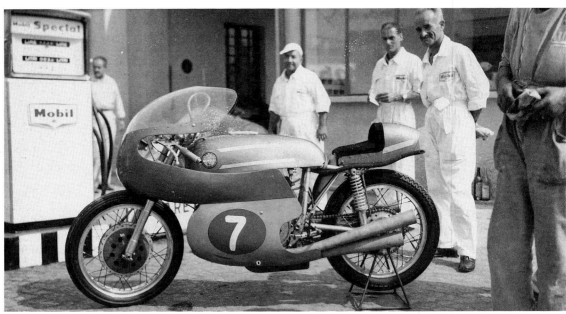

three laps due to carburettor trouble, Agostini broke the lap record to finish ninth. The Benelli '500' was fitted with a new twin-drum, double-leading-shoe front brake made by Ceriani.

Strange as it may seem, Benelli's biggest problem during 1967 was its riders, or lack of them. Now that it had four-cylinder machines for the 250, 350 and 500 cc classes, the Pesaro factory was handicapped by a shortage of pilots. Pasolini had been signed to replace Provini, and Amilcare Ballestrieri, a promising youngster, picked to support him. However, during practice for Modena, the first race of the Italian season, Ballestrieri crashed and was so shaken that he promptly decided to retire. This left lone

Right
Tarquinio Provini (left) shaking hands with Giovanni Benelli after signing for the Pesaro company at the end of 1963

Above
Provini working on his machine during practice week at the 1965 IoM TT

Below
Seen here in the 1965 TT race, Provini finished fourth at an average speed of 93.57 mph

hand 'Paso' having to compete by himself in all three classes!

It was mainly in the 350 class that Benelli shone that year, 'Paso' gaining several victories over Agostini in the shorter Italian races. In the Classics, however, 'Ago' and MV reigned supreme.

The burden of having to ride in three classes, together with the limited resources, continued to blunt Pasolini's challenge into 1968, although the Benelli rider scored a number of runner-up positions in the GPs: 250 cc (Isle of Man), 350 cc (West Germany, Isle of Man and Italy), 500 cc (Italy). Silvio Grassetti rejoined Benelli to provide extra support for the Italian Championships.

At Monza, in September 1968, Benelli wheeled out a pair of new 494.6 cc (54 × 54 mm) fours for Pasolini and Mike Hailwood. The latter had accepted an offer from Benelli after falling out over team orders from Count Agusta to 'let Agostini win both races' (350 and 500 cc).

During practice, Hailwood got to within a tenth of a second of the track record that he had set in the previous year with his works Honda four. However, in trying to keep up with Agostini's MV during a very wet race, he fell and was forced to retire. Meanwhile, Pasolini finished a safe second on the other machine.

After all the Japanese manufacturers had withdrawn, Benelli decided to concentrate on the 250 cc

This experimental twin-disc front brake was manufactured for Benelli by Bo Gehring of Harper's Ferry, West Virginia, May 1965

The 1967 16-valve 250 Benelli four, which produced almost 60 bhp. Shown without its fairing, the bike was ridden by Renzo Pasolini

Left

Pasolini in action on the 350 four-cylinder Benelli at Imola in May 1967. Like a similar 491 cc model, it sported a massive, double-sided, twin-leading-shoe front brake

world title chase in 1969 (the last year before the FIM's twin-cylinder, six-speed limit). In 1969 guise, the Benelli 250 four, now with eight speeds, produced 64 bhp at 14,500 rpm. Other changes included a 16-valve cylinder head and larger carburettors.

Pasolini looked capable of winning the title, but a couple of accidents, and the introduction of the Australian Kel Carruthers, meant that he was to finish fourth. Santiago Herrero (Ossa) was third, Kent Anderson (Yamaha TD2) second, while Carruthers scooped Benelli's second title to end the year as 250 cc World Champion. From this high point, Benelli created more rumour than results. Not only were several leading riders to be linked by the press with the company, but the Pesaro factory was often reputed to be working on a whole host of designs, including six-, eight- and even *nine*-cylinder devices!

Riders associated with Benelli included Phil Read, Jarno Saarinen and Hailwood (again!). All made an odd appearance on Benelli machinery during the late 1960s and early 1970s, but nothing permanent ever

'Paso' with one of his works Benellis at an Italian Senior Championship meeting, spring 1968. Note the Benelli 'lion' tank motif

Silvio Grassetti acted as support rider to Pasolini at some events during 1968. Here he is about to cast one of the 350 fours away in spectacular fashion at Cesenatico, in August that year

Above
The 1969 version of the 343.1 cc (51 × 42 mm) seven-speed four. It produced 64 bhp at 14,500 rpm

Below
Aussie Kel Carruthers on his way to victory in the 1969 250 cc TT. He went on to give Benelli its second world title

Carruthers and Benelli mechanics at Monza during training for the 1969 Italian GP. After joining the team in the Isle of Man, he was a consistent finisher in every championship round he contested that year

came of it. Silvio Grassetti and Walter Villa were another two who had occasional outings.

Then, after experiencing financial problems, the Benelli family sold its motorcycling operation to the Argentinian industrialist Alejandro de Tomaso, who had built up a number of lucrative businesses within the car industry.

At the time, it was reported that de Tomaso had purchased 85 per cent of Benelli shares. The remaining 15 per cent went to Marco and Luigi Benelli, sons of Giuseppe, one of the founder brothers.

One of de Tomaso's first moves (probably only a publicity venture) was to offer Giacomo Agostini some 70 million lire (almost £50,000 sterling at the prevailing exchange rate) to ride the Pesaro firm's latest machinery.

A month later, at the Milan show, Benelli ran MV close in attempting to get the most publicity (the Gallarate company had launched a Super Sport version of its 750 four roadster, which it claimed would do a *highly* optimistic 162 mph!). Benelli's tall story centred around the 'brand new' 500 cc four-cylinder racer, which formed the centrepiece of its show stand. The company *claimed* that it developed 100 bhp—Benelli representatives were not, however, sure of the engine's revs . . . .

Indeed, the engine was suspected to be merely the shell of one of the new, and slimmer, 500 cc units on which the Pesaro concern had been working intermittently for several years.

Certainly, the new Benelli was neatly designed and engineered. Its engine was very slim and compact, its frame well made and business like, and the light-alloy fairing a work of art. Observers raised the query as to whether it would ever be raced and, if so, by whom. Factory staff would not commit themselves beyond : 'Possibly in 1973'.

The claim was partly true, because Walter Villa did race a revamped 350 Benelli four in the 1973 Italian GP at Monza, but that was truly the marque's final Grand Prix appearance. Thus, the Benelli racing chapter came to an end. It had been dominated by two engine formats—the double-knocker single and across-the-frame four—both world champions in their day.

3
Bianchi

Founded by Edoardo Bianchi in Milan, during 1885, the company which bore his name was destined to become the very first to manufacture motorcycles in Italy. Versatility was its keynote in those early days; first came surgical instruments, then bicycles, trikes and finally, in 1897, motorcycles.

However, it was not until 1920 that the Milanese company began to take a serious interest in speed events. It was in that year that Carlo Maffeis, riding a 500 cc V-twin ohv Bianchi, established a new flying kilometre world record at 77.6 mph, on a stretch of road near Gallarate (later the home of the legendary MV Agusta marque). Even then, it was not a full works effort, as the engine had been prepared by Carlo and his brothers, Miro and Nando, who later marketed their own Maffeis machine powered by British JAP and Blackburne engines. Riding his record-breaking V-twin Bianchi in the following year's Brescia road races, Carlo Maffeis crashed heavily and died of his injuries.

Following this tragedy, Bianchi took no further part in racing until 1925, when it became necessary to counter the challenge being made to its sales by the likes of Moto Guzzi and Garelli. Both companies were winning races and, thus, gaining valuable publicity which, of course, was being denied Bianchi. Initially, Bianchi chose to dispute the 350 cc class which, in Italy, was dominated by the all-conquering Garelli two-stroke split-single.

The new Bianchi was designed by Ing. Mario Baldi and incorporated several original features, which were highly regarded by rival manufacturers, both in Italy and overseas.

Baldi's design featured a 74 mm bore and 81 mm stroke, giving a capacity of 348 cc. It had double overhead camshafts, driven by a bevel shaft and spur gears. A rarity in those days was that the camshafts and coil valve springs were completely enclosed in an oiltight compartment. The engine developed 24 bhp (eventually raised to 30 bhp) at

5000 rpm and had a compression ratio of 5:5:1. The timing gear was on the offside of the power unit, while on the nearside, the crankshaft carried two sprockets. The inner sprocket provided the drive, via a fully-enclosed chain, to the magneto; the outer sprocket drove the exposed simplex primary drive chain, which was lubricated by a drip-feed system.

Lubrication was by the dry-sump method, in which a gear-type pump was used, there being a separate oil tank beneath the seat. There was also an auxiliary oil supply to the overhead camshafts, effected by a hand-operated plunger pump that drew its supply from a small tank carried atop the fuel tank. A multi-plate dry clutch transmitted the power output to a three-speed gearbox, in semi-unit with the crankcase, and there was the period tank-mounted lever and quadrant for gear changing.

Named the *Freccia Celeste* (Blue Arrow), this machine proved not only very fast, but also extremely reliable. It won the long-distance Milano-Taranto, the ultra-demanding Lario race, and the Italian Grand Prix over the Monza Autodrome speed bowl.

The legendary Tazio Nuvolari, who had begun his career aboard Garelli two-strokes, was recruited into the Bianchi squad, which also included the likes of Varzi, Arcangeli and Moretti. Nuvolari made his Bianchi début at the 1925 Italian GP, where he was forced to take a position at the back of the grid with a pusher, being hampered with a plaster cast following a car accident he had suffered on the same circuit in the previous week. Undismayed, Nuvolari overtook the entire field to win the race at record speed— faster, in fact, than the majority of the 500s!

From that moment on, until the end of 1930, the Bianchi double-knocker totally monopolized the 350 cc class in Italy. It eclipsed the Garellis and any British machines which put in an appearance.

Nuvolari won the Italian GP again in 1926, 1927 and 1928, only missing out in 1929 when lubrication

trouble set in after he had become the first man on a 350 to raise the Monza lap record to over 90 mph. Even so, another Bianchi, ridden by Moretti, went on to win.

A run of Nuvolari victories in the Lario race was interrupted only in 1928, when his great Bianchi rival, Achille Varzi, won. Nuvolari had experienced wheel problems (spoke breakages) after riding with particular force (the Lario event was staged over largely unmade surfaces, which were the ultimate test of a wheelbuilder's art).

By the end of 1930, the *Freccia Celeste* had had its day. Even with the advantage of a four-speed gearbox, it could no longer match the top foreign machines, such as the British Norton and Swiss Motosacoche.

During the mid 1950s, Bianchi concentrated its efforts upon motocross and long-distance races. Works rider Gianfranco Muscio is shown, during 1956, on one of the specially-prepared 175 cc ohc singles

After its run of success, Bianchi had no desire to quit the racing scene, so Ing. Baldi went back to his drawing office, and in 1932 the result of this work made its début. It was, in effect, an enlarged 350. The step up to 500 cc was achieved with the all-new 82 mm bore and 94 mm stroke dimensions, which provided 33 bhp at 5000 rpm. Early models sported a rigid frame, like the 350, but later versions were equipped with plunger rear suspension.

The 500, dohc, single-cylinder Bianchi proved as sturdy and reliable as its forebear, making it an ideal mount for the tough long-distance races of the day.

In 1933 Pigorini won the Milano-Napoli event at an average speed of almost 60 mph; Fumagalli won the 1934 Lario race, while Serafina took the same event in the following year. However, in Grand Prix events, Bianchi found the going much more difficult, as its machine simply was not fast enough against the likes of the latest Norton singles or Guzzi's new V-twin, let alone the four-cylinder Rondine from which the Gilera was developed.

It was against this background that Bianchi instructed Ing. Baldi to design a brand-new multi-cylinder machine. The result was the breathtaking, supercharged 500 cc four-cylinder model which first appeared towards the end of 1938. Baldi's creation differed from other Italian fours of the period—the Gilera and Benelli—in having *vertical* cylinders instead of inclined units and relying upon air instead of liquid for cooling.

In 1957 Bianchi switched its efforts by constructing a fully-streamlined record-breaker, which established two world speed records at Monza in November of that year. Riders were Alano Montanari and Gino Franzosi. Running on alcohol, the 175 cc engine gave 17 bhp at 8000 rpm

The twin overhead camshafts were driven by a single bevel shaft at the offside of the engine, instead of by a gear train accommodated between the middle cylinders. Bore and stroke dimensions were 52×58 mm, while the power output of the engine, which featured magneto ignition and a gear-driven supercharger, was in the region of 75 bhp at 9000 rpm. It had a four-speed transmission and chain final drive, together with a truly massive frame, which had plunger rear suspension and blade-type girder front forks. Sadly, before development had been completed, this highly interesting machine was mothballed because of the outbreak of World War 2.

By the time hostilities finally came to an end, Ing. Baldi had died and the FIM had banned supercharging. These two events dealt the Bianchi four a terminal blow.

For a time, during the immediate post-war period, the only Bianchi sporting activity was limited participation in trials with 125 cc two-strokes. Then came motocross and long-distance races, the factory-supported riders using much the same models as the 174 and 205 cc ohv and ohc four-stroke production machines then being marketed by the Milanese company. Bianchi gained several successes in the

Above
Production-based 203 cc Bianchi, as ridden in 1959–60 by journalist/racer Roberto Patrignani, who is shown here with the bike

Below
A similar machine to Patrignani's, but with Oldani twin-leading-shoe front brake. It was raced by Horace Crowder and Derek Minter on British short circuits in the early 1960s

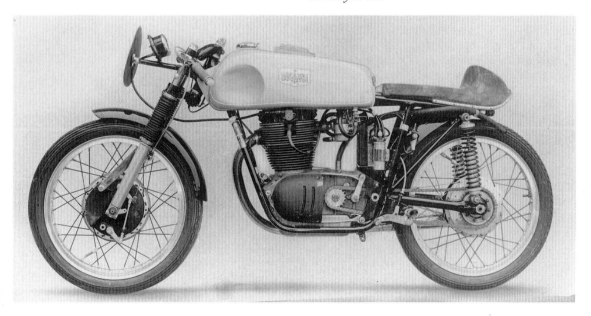

Bianchi made a dramatic return to Grand Prix racing in 1960 with a number of 248 cc dohc twins designed by Lino Tonti. The Milanese team is shown here during its unsuccessful visit to the IoM TT that year. Derek Minter (seated on the nearest bike) was a member of the squad

Milano-Taranto, the Giro d'Italia and various hill-climbs; it also won the Italian Motocross Championship in 1958, 1959 and 1960.

In addition, Bianchi had received world-wide publicity when, in November 1957, it took two world speed records at Monza, using a fully-streamlined 175 machine derived from the production ohc Tonale. Running on alcohol, with a compression ratio of 10:1, power output of the machine's engine was 17 bhp at 8000 rpm.

Prepared by Ing. Columbo (formerly with Gilera), the streamliner was ridden by Alano Montanari and Gino Franzosi. The pair broke both the 1000-kilometre and hour records for the class, but poor weather ruined further attempts on several other medium- and long-distance speeds. The 1000-kilometre record was achieved in 5 hours, 23 minutes, 9.8 seconds at 115.37 mph, and the hour at 115.47 mph.

Ing. Columbo also prepared a 235 cc (66 × 66 mm) engine for racing events, but results in Italy were never anything to get excited about. However, this machine eventually found its way to Britain. Owned by Peter Doncaster, it was raced on the short circuits with considerable success in the period 1960–2 by first Horace Crowder and then Derek Minter.

In mid 1958 Ing. Lino Tonti became the head of the Bianchi racing and development department. Tonti, who had previously been with Aermacchi, Mondial and Paton, immediately got down to the task of designing a new quarter-litre engine which could be used for either road racing or motocross.

First came the off-roader. It made a promising start at the Italian round of the Coupe d'Europe at Pinerolo; later, ridden by the likes of Soletti, Caroli and Ostenero, it went on to scoop three Italian championship titles.

The tarmac version made its début at the non-championship Swiss GP at Locarno. Gianfranco Muscio raced it with favourable results, despite persistent valve-spring problems which eventually forced him to retire.

There were also 175 cc versions, which were very similar, except for bore and stroke dimensions, and intended for Italian use.

The oversquare power units, 65 × 52.6 mm (174 cc) and 77 × 53.4 mm (248 cc) had twin overhead cams and fully-enclosed valve gear (essential in its off-road role, where dust and mud would have played havoc). In road racing form, the 175 gave 20 bhp at 10,500 rpm, and the 250 30 bhp at 10,000 rpm. The motocrosser had a slightly lower output at lower rpm because higher torque was needed.

Primary drive was by gears, running with the multi-plate clutch in an oil-bath on the nearside of the heavily-finned crankcases. The power was

Frame from a 1960 250 twin. Note the use of small-diameter tubing and the twin-cylinder ignition coil

Ing. Tonti soon enlarged the capacity of the Bianchi twin to 348.4 cc (70 × 59 mm). This first appeared in late 1960 and was much more competitive than the original smaller model. Early races, however, were blighted by a series of mechanical problems

Overleaf
The great Scot Bob McIntyre had been sufficiently impressed by the 350 Bianchi twin to sign for the company to race the machine in the 1961 World Championship series. Bob 'Mac' is shown displaying his own aggressive style in the Ulster GP that year

transmitted via a five-speed gearbox in unit with the engine.

The two coils for the twin-spark ignition were attached to the front tubes of the duplex cradle frame, which had conventional twin-shock, swinging-arm suspension at the rear and oil-damped teles up front. Brakes were Oldani drums, a 220 mm unit at the front, and a 180 mm assembly at the rear.

On the last day of March 1960, the Bianchi factory held a dinner for the press corps in Milan, dropping something of a bombshell by announcing a major thrust for Grand Prix honours. This was to be made with a works team mounted on a brand-new 250 cc twin-cylinder model, claimed to produce 34 bhp at 11,500 rpm.

The new machine, which Ing. Tonti had designed and built over the preceding winter months, comprised a vertical twin engine built in unit with a six-speed gearbox and mounted in a 9 kg (20 lb) welded duplex frame. The last featured extensive triangulation.

Supported in two ball and two roller bearings, the built-up crankshaft assembly included four flywheel discs. Between the inner pair was a pinion, from which both transmission and valve gear were driven. The pinion meshed with a gear on an intermediate shaft, at the nearside end of which was another gear driving the exposed dry clutch; the final drive was taken from the offside of the unit. A train of gears, housed in an upward extension of the crankcase between the cylinders, transferred the drive from the intermediate gear to the inlet camshaft, while a further train led forward from there to the exhaust camshaft.

Electron alloy was employed for the cam boxes, clutch housing and integral 2.25-litre (½-gallon) sump; the crankcase, cylinder barrels and heads were in aluminium alloy. Each head featured dual 12 mm spark plugs, which fired simultaneously courtesy of a pair of Bosch six-volt, double-ended coils, which were mounted just aft of the steering head.

There were a total of *four* contact-breakers, which

Remo Venturi signed for Bianchi in 1963. Here a works mechanic holds his 350 mount during the Italian GP at Monza, where Venturi came home third behind Redman (Honda) and Shepherd (MZ)

were driven by the offside end of the crankshaft. With a bore and stroke of 55 × 52.5 mm, the engine was slightly oversquare. Twin 27 mm Dell'Orto carburettors were of the SS1 variety with separate float chambers. Two oil pumps were used; one fed the crankshaft bearings, the other the valve gear.

There was a strong family resemblance between the frame and that of the successful motocross models. However, some of the triangulated tubes on the racer were smaller in diameter, while there was an additional, oval-section tube connecting the top of the steering head to a crossmember at the seat nose.

Equipped with a quick-release cap and twin large-bore taps, the 14-litre (3-gallon) petrol tank was a superbly-crafted affair in aluminium alloy. The Bianchi motif was proudly displayed on its sides.

The front forks were specially commissioned and were interesting in two respects. Firstly, the top and bottom yokes were made of light alloy; secondly, the wheel spindle was mounted in lugs extending forwards from the sliders (this arrangement permitted straighter, stiffer yokes). Both the front and rear suspension assemblies were manufactured for Bianchi by the Ceriani company.

Other details included 18 in. wheels, Oldani twin-leading-shoe brakes with a diameter of 200 mm, and a purpose-built aluminium fairing, which had seven bonded-rubber attachments riveted in place. Dry weight was 127 kg (280 lb).

Riders were named as Osvaldo Perfetti, Gianfranco Muscio and the Englishman Derek Minter.

Much was expected of the Bianchi effort, but due to a series of mechanical problems, which centred around the caged-roller big-end bearings and gearbox, finishes, let alone results, were at a premium. However, this did not stop Ing. Tonti from proceeding apace with development. By the time the Italian GP, at Monza, rolled around in September 1960, a 348.4 cc (65 × 52.5 mm) version made its début. Ridden by Muscio and Ernesto Brambilla, the 'new' 350 Bianchis really harried the MV fours in the early laps, before engine vibration put paid to Brambilla's chances, while a broken oil pipe sidelined Muscio.

In January 1961 the former Gilera star Bob McIntyre visited Italy, at the invitation of Bianchi, to test ride its latest works machines. The tests took place at the Modena Autodrome, near Bologna, as there were icy patches on the Monza circuit. Afterwards, McIntyre said, 'I rode the 350 twin and it was very good. I was impressed, it's certainly faster than any British 350, but like anything Italian, it's rather temperamental.'

By mid March, after another try-out, this time at Monza, McIntyre finally said yes.

Bianchi's first victory with one of the twin-cylinder models came on 3 April 1961, when Ernesto

Brambilla won the 500 cc class of the second round of the Italian Senior Championship at Cesenatico, on the Adriatic Coast. Brambilla, on the latest 350 works machine, had no difficulty in beating Libero Liberati (Gilera Saturno), who finished second after a dice with Gilberto Milani on another Bianchi, which terminated when Milani went out with a broken chain.

The first round of the 1961 World Championship took place at the very fast Hockenheim circuit, in West Germany. Much was expected of McIntyre and Brambilla in the 350 cc race, but after showing early promise, both soon retired—McIntyre with piston trouble and Brambilla with an ignition fault.

Next came the Isle of Man TT. Here Brambilla decided to 'save my engine for the next round' (the Dutch TT). Instead, Bianchi had McIntyre plus fellow Scot Alastair King.

McIntyre started off in fine style, too, and at Ginger Hall, he was already ten seconds up on second-placed Hocking with the MV four. That was

Bianchi works bikes at Monza, 15 September 1963. Note the differing designs of front fork. By then, reliability was much improved

For the 1964 season, Ing. Tonti created a full-blown 500—498.1 cc (73 × 59.5 mm). It pumped out a claimed 72 bhp and finally provided Bianchi with a competitive bike for the all-important 500 cc class

as far as he got, however, as he struck yet more piston trouble. The other Bianchi runner, King, also retired—this time at Ballacraine, on the second lap, with a broken gearbox mainshaft.

After these performances, one would have given little chance of a Bianchi actually finishing the Dutch TT at Assen, let alone challenging for the lead throughout the gruelling 20-lap, 95.75-mile race, but that is exactly what transpired. Bob McIntyre and MV team leader Gary Hocking fought tooth and nail for the lead. *The Motor Cycle* commented that 'Mac appeared to have the steam, but Hocking's youthful verve snatched back precious inches on the swervery and left the crowd reeling.'

At the line, Hocking made a titanic effort, snatching victory by a couple of machine lengths; Brambilla was fourth. This was the first time that Bianchi had shown real promise with the new design at the top level.

The improved reliability continued at the Sachsenring, in East Germany, where McIntyre came third and Brambilla fifth. Then came what many considered Bianchi's best hope of success that year—the Ulster GP. Unfortunately, a combination of handling problems and a recurrence of gearbox troubles, which eliminated McIntyre half-way through, saw to that. Even so, Alastair King finished in the runner-up spot, 40 seconds behind race winner Hocking.

The biggest technical surprise at Monza, for the Italian GP in early September, came when the Bianchi camp turned up with a 386 cc twin (a 350 bored out to 68.4 mm) with *four* carburettors. Ing. Tonti stated that the idea of this purely experimental set-up was 'to improve acceleration'. The two instruments per cylinder fed through conventional single inlet valves—notably, the two outside carburettors were *smaller* than the inside ones (20 mm compared to 25 mm).

In all, Bianchi had six machines at Monza—five 350s and the prototype 386 cc model. The latter was used in the final practice session by Paddy Driver, but after misfiring badly, it was not raced. Driver rode a 350 together with Alan Shepherd and

Remo Venturi in action with the 500 at Modena in March 1964, when he scored a sensational victory, defeating the combined might of the MV Agusta and Gilera teams

'regular' Bianchi men McIntyre, King and Brambilla, but only Shepherd finished—back in fourth behind Hocking and Hailwood (MVs) and Havel (Jawa).

In 1962 the situation was rather quiet for Bianchi. After originally being keen to continue riding for the Milanese concern, McIntyre opted instead to become a works Honda rider, whilst Brambilla and new signing Silvio Grassetti mainly concentrated their efforts at home. Even so, Grassetti did gain a couple of third places in the classics (Holland and Italy).

Ing. Tonti had continued development of both the 350 and the over-bored version for 500 cc events, and in February 1963 came news that ex-MV teamster Remi Venturi had signed on the dotted line to race for Bianchi in both the Italian and World Championship series that year.

With the power of the smaller twin increased to

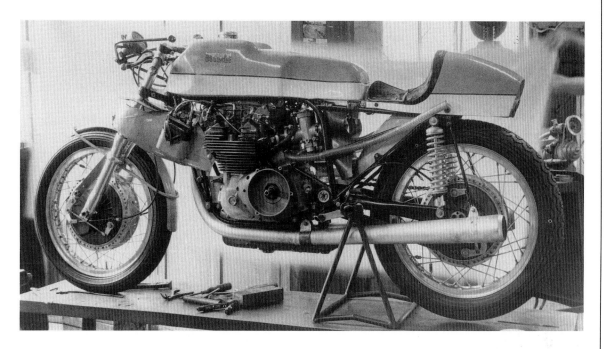

The 1964 498 cc Bianchi twin, minus its streamlining and clutch. Its full potential was not to be realized due to financial problems at the Milan factory, which led to the works racers being sold off to privateers in Italy and Germany

53 bhp at 10,800 rpm, Venturi put up some outstanding performances, including second at the West German GP and a string of wins and places in Italy. The highlight was victory in the Shell Gold Cup at Imola.

Venturi also proved a real threat on the 386 cc model. After putting the 500 MVs of Grassetti and Shepherd under pressure at Modena in March, Venturi benefited by Tonti's further enlargement of the engine to a 68 mm bore and longer stroke of 56 mm to give 422 cc. This was followed by 440 cc (69 × 56 mm) and 454 cc (70 × 59 mm). The latter capacity provided 59 bhp at 10,000 rpm.

This success spurred Ing. Tonti to create a full-blown 500 with bore and stroke of 73 × 59.5 mm, giving an exact capacity of 498.1 cc. His efforts were rewarded at Modena in March 1964, when Venturi scored a sensational victory by defeating both the MV and Gilera teams!

The full 500 produced a claimed 72 bhp at 10,200 rpm and provided good power from as low as 6000 rpm. This wide power-band, coupled with a six-speed gearbox, made the Bianchi relatively easy to ride. The biggest problem was wheelspin

during acceleration (only a 3.50 section rear tyre was employed).

Where Venturi also scored, particularly on a dry track, was in the braking department. Over the winter, Bianchi had developed its own twin-leading-shoe brakes. All three—there were two on the front wheel, mounted side by side—were of the same dimensions; 230 mm (9.5 in.) in diameter by 30 mm (1.25 in.) wide. The frame had also received attention, and handling and roadholding were now up to MV standards.

Venturi continued to dominate the Italian scene, winning the 1964 500 cc Senior Championship title. Although less successful in the classics, none the less he impressed, particularly at the Dutch TT, where the Bianchi rider was third (350) and second (500).

However, the whole future of the racing effort, and the factory itself, was under threat. By July creditors were beginning to gather, as a string of unpaid bills began to surface. The result was a court-appointed administrator who halted the race effort, while Ing. Tonti quit.

This effectively was the end. Although Grassetti rode privately-entered machines to some success in 1965, the majority of the bikes and spares were sold off to private buyers in Italy and Germany at the end of 1964 to raise much-needed capital.

Bianchi struggled along for a couple more years, producing its range of small-capacity roadsters, but the days of racing glory were at an end.

4

Ducati

In pre-war days, the Ducati company was involved primarily in the manufacture of electrical equipment. This meant that when Italy joined the hostilities in June 1940, the Bologna company's production was switched to radio transmitters and the like for military use.

After the conflict, Ducati's vast production facilities lay idle, with countless workers laid off. This, in turn, led to a reformed organization headed by a partnership between the Italian government and the Vatican. One of the company's first moves was to take on board the design of an auxiliary 48 cc four-stroke engine for fitment to conventional pedal cycles, or for sale to existing moped manufacturers.

The first complete Ducati motorcycle, powered by

a 60 cc engine, appeared in 1950. Some two years later, Ducati split into two completely separate commercial companies. One concentrated on electrical equipment; the other moved into new premises next door to carry out the design and construction of powered two-wheelers, together with small-capacity diesel engines. This latter concern was known as Ducati Meccanica.

Established manufacturers thought this an unwise move, as there was already excess production capacity within the industry. However, those critics had reckoned without the man charged to carry through these bold plans to fruition—Dott. Giuseppe Montano. He had been appointed general manager upon the foundation of the separate motorcycle plant.

Dott. Montano at once saw that the way to publicize the name Ducati was to race and win. He reached this view after examining the problem from a distance, as he was strictly a business executive, not a racing enthusiast.

With this policy decision taken, Montano had to find a suitable engineer with whom he could entrust the design and development of machinery capable of winning races. He found just such a man in a former Ceccato and Mondial engineer, Ing. Fabio Taglioni, who subsequently joined the Bologna company on 1 May 1954.

As the Ducati company was mainly interested in sports racing at that time, Ing. Taglioni began by designing a single-cylinder, single-overhead-camshaft, 98.058 cc (49 × 52 mm) model, which was officially called the Gran Sport, but soon earned the nickname 'Marianna'. Sturdily constructed and offered at an affordable price (at least in Italy), it

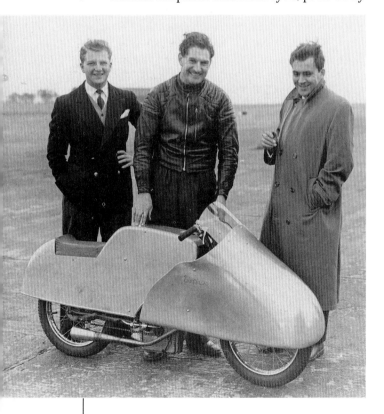

Smiling faces hide a distinct lack of 'go' for the 50 cc Britax Hurricane, shown here in February 1955. Its alloy streamlining hid a tuned Ducati Cucciolo clip-on, pull-rod engine, which was hard-pressed to propel the bike beyond 50 mph

The first 'real' Ducati racer was the Taglioni-conceived 98 cc Gran Sport with bevel-driven ohc engine, circa 1955

was fast, reliable and easy to maintain. Like the subsequent 125 cc version, it sold in quite large quantities, both in Italy and abroad (something like 350 units combined of the 98 and 125 cc models).

Its first racing airing came early in the 1955 season, when a number of factory-backed entrants packed their class leader-board in both the Milano-Taranto and Giro d'Italia long-distance marathons.

An initial power output of 9 bhp at 9000 rpm, with the engine running on an 8:5:1 compression ratio, was later boosted to 12 bhp at 10,500 rpm. As a result, the maximum speed rose from 80 to 87 mph. The larger version was achieved by simply boring out the cylinder to 55.5 mm, giving a capacity of 124.558 cc.

In both versions, the engine was a supremely neat and compact unit-construction device with a single overhead camshaft, exposed rockers and hairpin valve springs. The light-alloy cylinder, with cast-iron liner, was inclined 10 degrees forward; there was an alloy cylinder head with 80-degree valve angles and a separate cambox (unlike the later models); and the crankcases were split vertically. The straight-cut primary drive and wet multi-plate clutch were on the nearside, transmitting power to a four-speed, close-ratio gearbox. The crankshaft, with full-circle flywheels, carried a flywheel-mounted generator on its drive-side end, supplying current for the 6-volt battery of the coil ignition system; at the opposite end, outside the timing bevel, a gear with straight-cut teeth provided the drive for the oil pump and also for the contact-breaker. Adjustment of the points could be made through a spring-retained inspection cap at the front of the crankcase timing cover.

The overhead camshaft was driven by vertical

Ing. Fabio Taglioni designed this 175 cc twin-cylinder engine for events such as the Milano-Taranto and Giro d'Italia marathons. It made its public début at the Milan show in November 1956

Production Ducati 125 Grand Prix dohc engine, which was very similar to the works Desmo unit, with the exception of the cylinder head

drive shafts and bevel gears—with a split Oldhams coupling half-way up the side of the cylinder barrel. The crankshaft was equipped with a replaceable connecting rod, which featured a caged-roller-bearing big-end and phosphor-bronze bush small-end. There was wet-sump lubrication. Throughout the engine, the castings and materials were of particularly high quality.

If anything, the Gran Sport was over-engineered, not only making it very suitable for the long-distance road events of the era, but also as the basis of ever-increasing capacity enlargements as time went by (culminating in 435.661 cc—86 × 76 mm—in 1969). Except for the pure racing components, such as a double-webbed con-rod, straight-cut primary gears, high-compression forged piston, separate cambox, exposed valve gear and a few smaller details, it was essentially the same as the roadgoing singles which soon followed.

Likewise, the frame and the rest of the running gear acted as prototypes for what was to come later. The frame consisted of an open-cradle, single-downtube design with the engine forming an integral stress member.

Other technical details of this first Taglioni Ducati design included a Dell'Orto SS1 racing carburettor, fully-enclosed front and rear suspension, single-leading-shoe conical brake hubs, alloy wheel rims,

an 18-litre alloy petrol tank, single 'bum-stop' racing saddle, and a long, shallow-taper megaphone exhaust that gave a deep bellowing note.

The 98 cc engine was also put into a special one-off, record-breaking streamliner which, ridden by Mario Carini and Sandro Cireri at Monza in November 1956, established 44 new world speed records. These included the hour for machines up to 175 cc at 101 mph.

The 125 cc single-knocker was developed into the Formula 3 model, with more power and enclosed valve gear, while a new 125 cc double-overhead-cam engine was built for a batch of special Grand Prix machines. These were the first proper Ducati racers to enter international events, and they made their début in early 1956.

However, it was the desmodromic version, with its positive valve closing and opening mechanism that really put the Ducati name on the racing map. Ing. Taglioni worked away on this design throughout the spring and early summer of 1956, before factory rider Degli Antoni gave the prototype a victorious début in the Swedish GP at Hedemora in July that year. In fact, not only did he win the race, but he lapped the entire field at least once in the process!

Race début for Taglioni's masterpiece, the 125 Desmo single, came at the Swedish GP on 15 July 1956. Rider Degli Antoni not only won the race, but lapped the entire field at least once in the process

When one realizes that the desmodromic valve
layout was a project that had already defeated some
of the best brains in motorcycle racing—in fact, the
only company to make a *successful* desmo racing
power-unit before Ducati was the giant Mercedes-
Benz organization in the car world—it is a tribute
to Taglioni's engineering skill that he created a successful racing version. However, he also went on to
create a production variant—Ducati is still the only
company to have offered this to its customers.

Development of new roadgoing models meant that
the Taglioni desmo single racer was not able to compete on a regular basis until the 1958 season. The
rival MV Agusta concern had the two finest lightweight riders in Carlo Ubbiali and Tarquinio Provini. None the less, the Bologna factory signed up
the ex-Gilera star Romolo Ferri and ex-MV teamster
Luigi Taveri. Alberto Gandossi, who was already a
rider for Ducati, was retained, while Dave Chadwick

*The 125 Desmo single-cylinder engine. Capable of over
110 mph, the bike could be fitted with a five- or six-
speed gearbox, depending on the circuit*

*Leading British rider/dealer Fron Purslow acquired
one of the works Desmo singles (fitted with a valve-
spring head) in early 1958,* Motor Cycle *journalist Vic
Willoughby is shown leading on the Ducati, with
Purslow shadowing him on an NSU Sportmax. The
location is Sleap Airfield, Shrewsbury*

and Sammy Miller signed on for the first classic, the Isle of Man TT.

In this event, Taveri challenged the MV riders all the way until he was forced out with piston trouble; then Ferri took up the challenge to finish second, Chadwick third and Miller fourth. At the Dutch TT, Taveri was only beaten by a length, and at the Belgian GP came the first Ducati win that year when Gandossi crossed the line first, followed by Ferri. The German GP at the Nürburgring proved disastrous: Ferri crashed and broke several bones, while Taveri and Gandossi both went out with mechanical trouble within a few miles of each other.

The company was not disheartened, however, and the very next weekend, at Hedemora, Gandossi and

Above
By 1958 Ducati was ready for a crack at the 125 cc world title. It signed a number of riders, including the ex-Gilera lightweight star Romolo Ferri, shown here in the IoM TT. Ferri finished second behind race winner Ubbiali

Left
Another member of the 1958 Ducati squad was the Swiss rider Luigi Taveri. Here Taveri (8) leads MV teamsters Ubbiali (1) and Provini (2) during the 125 cc Dutch TT

Above right
The crankshaft and piston from the 125 Ducati Desmo single

Right
Amadora double-sided front brake of the 125 Desmo single. The same unit was also fitted to the 125 GP and 175 F3 production racers

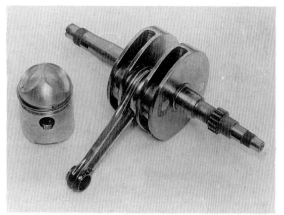

Taveri scored a brilliant 1–2 in the Swedish Grand Prix. At the Ulster GP, they took second, third and fourth (after Gandossi had led in the early stages before falling) and then, at Monza, came a smashing first *five* places, which had the MV team reeling on the ropes!

In its first full year of Grand Prix competition, Ducati scored three victories in seven events and made the fastest lap in five!

The final round at Monza had seen the début of a new 124.50 cc (42.5 × 45 mm) twin-cylinder racer, again with desmodromic valve gear, driven by a chain of gears accommodated between the two cylinders. With a compression ratio of 10:2:1, the engine developed a claimed 22.5 bhp at 13,800 rpm and could be allowed to touch 17,000 rpm on the over-run without disaster. The twin had coil ignition, each cylinder being fired by a single 10 mm spark plug. A six-speed gearbox was needed to keep the tiny pistons spinning within their optimum power-band.

The five Monza finishers consisted of the winner, Bruno Spaggiari, plus Alberto Gandossi, Francesco Villa (riding the new twin), Dave Chadwick and Luigi Taveri.

Spaggiari, Gandossi and Taveri were joined for the 1959 season by the up-and-coming young Mike Hailwood, whose father, Stan, headed the new British importers, Ducati Concessionaires. However, continual bad luck made what promised to be a great season for Ducati just the reverse. There was only

Left
A twin-cylinder 125 Desmo made its début in the 1958 Italian GP. Intended as a replacement for the single, it proved overweight and underpowered

Right
Mike Hailwood's 250 Desmo twin at a Silverstone test session in April 1960. A race winner on the British short circuits, it could not repeat this success on the world stage

Below
P. J. Bidder, on a 125 Ducati F3, leads D. Holden, on an MV Agusta, during the 150 cc final at Rhydymwyn road races, 3 June 1961

Above
John Surtees acquired the majority of the Hailwood and Kavanagh Desmo twins. Here Ray Brittain (left) and Ken Sprayston, of Reynolds Tubes, look on as Norman Surtees (kneeling) studies their handiwork, February 1962

one Grand Prix victory—in Ulster, where Hailwood got home on one of the singles. As for the twin, the best it could do all season was a repeat of its Monza third place, this time with Taveri in the saddle.

Discouraged with these results and suffering from a recession in the sales of its production roadsters, Ducati withdrew from racing at the end of 1959. The desmos were sold off to the leading riders, both in Italy and abroad, among them Mike Hailwood, who enjoyed considerable success with the singles during the following summer on British short circuits. In 1961 Franco Farne, with another of the singles, won the first three rounds of the Italian Senior Championship and the 125 cc class of the international *Coppa de Shell* (Shell Gold Cup) at Imola. In the latter, he fought all the way to the flag with Ernst Degner (MZ) and Tom Phillis and Jim Redman on Hondas. After those successes, however, Farne was laid low for a long spell as the result of a crash.

Taglioni designed this jewel-like 125 four-cylinder racer in 1960. Unfortunately, it was not ready until 1965, by which time, the Japanese had put their big-budget effort into overdrive and the Ducati was outclassed

For the vast majority, Ducati racing 1960s-style meant cheap and cheerful race-prepared roadsters. Typical was this 248 cc Vic Camp Mach 1, being ridden to victory at Cadwell Park on 12 September 1966 by John Kirkby

In 1960 Ducati built larger-capacity—247.7 cc (55.25 × 52 mm) and 348 cc (64 × 54 mm)—twin-cylinder desmos for Mike Hailwood and Ken Kavannagh respectively. Later, Stan Hailwood also acquired examples of the larger twin for his son Mike to ride.

Unfortunately, these machines were little more than prototypes and were afflicted with a variety of problems, although the 350 offered an excellent power-to-weight ratio when it appeared. Another problem of the 250 and 350 twins was their less-than-perfect roadholding. This led to a number of special frames being commissioned; these were built by both Ernie Earles and Reynolds Tubes. Leading-link front forks from the latter concern were also used on some machines.

In the view of the author, the various parallel twins were never given the factory development which they required to transform them into truly race-worthy motorcycles. After being campaigned by a number of riders, they were destined to grow less and less competitive as the years rolled by.

Of more benefit and more lasting use were the over-the-counter racers, which Ducati built and sold during the late 1950s and early 1960s, in the shape of the 175 and 250 Formula 3 sohc singles. The 174 cc

Above

The V-twin revived Ducati's fortunes in the 1970s.
This is one of ten works 750 cc engines built for the
Imola 200 in 1972. Ducati scored first and second
places, thanks to Paul Smart and Bruno Spaggiari

Above left

A factory mechanic works on one of the two 500
V-twins which Ducati sent to Silverstone in August
1971. They were ridden by Phil Read and Bruno
Spaggiari

Left

Works rider and factory tester Bruno Spaggiari rode
singles and V-twins to numerous victories over a
period of almost 20 years. Among them was the
Barcelona 24-hour race at Montjuich Park

Overleaf

The legendary Mike Hailwood during his winning
comeback ride on a Ducati 900 V-twin during the
1978 IoM TT

(62 × 57.8 mm) and 248 cc (74 × 57.8 mm) F3s were produced in limited quantities, but these capacities—together with 203 cc (67 × 57.8 mm), 340 cc (76 × 75 mm) and 436 cc (86 × 75 mm) versions—were converted from roadsters into race-kitted clubman racers at budget prices through the years. In fact, these 'home-brewed' Ducatis currently account for a considerable percentage of any entry in today's classic racing scene, providing cheap, reliable sport compared to the far more specialized machines, which are expensive in the extreme.

After Ducati quit GP racing, and stopped offering 'real' racers for sale, at the beginning of the 1960s, all the subsequent *factory* racers of the Bologna marque were built primarily to test new designs, rather than to achieve publicity, as was the case with, say, MV Agusta and Gilera.

Under that heading, I would include the various Barcelona 24-hour endurance racing successes gained by both singles and V-twin models; the 250, 350 and 450 production-based Desmo singles raced by Bruno Spaggiari during the late 1970s in Italy; the Imola V-twins of the 1972–4 period; Mike Hailwood's victorious return to the Isle of Man TT in 1978 aboard a 900 V-twin; and the Four of Formula

TT2 World Championships achieved by Tony Rutter in the early 1980s.

For the purpose of this book, Ducati's real works racing challenge for Grand Prix success came over only one season, and that was 1958.

Virginio Ferrari partnered Benjimin Grau on this works NCR 900 V-twin at Barcelona in July 1976. Ducati was the most successful marque in this world-famous event, gaining a string of wins over the years

5
Gilera

Any racing history of the Gilera marque is bound to concentrate upon an engine which changed the course of the motorcycle itself, the across-the-frame four-cylinder.

The Gilera *quattro* (four) has its origins in the year 1923. It was then that two young Rome engineers, Carlo Gianini and Piero Remor, designed and built a 490 cc (51 × 60 mm) engine with a single overhead camshaft, which was driven by a train of gears set between two pairs of cylinders.

The following year, joined by another motorcycle

This pre-war 500 Gilera watercooled, supercharged four was used by Nello Pagani to win the 1946 Swiss GP, which was held over the tricky Bremgarten circuit in Berne

enthusiast in Rome, Count Giovanni Bonmartini, they produced their first complete machine—the GRB, named from a gathering of their initials. Development of this machine continued until 1928, by which time, it was producing around 28 bhp at 6000 rpm.

An aircooled unit up to then, the engine was modified by having the exhaust zone and the area around each sparking plug cooled by water. Power output was boosted to 32 bhp at 6500 rpm.

Two years on and the whole GRB project was in grave danger of folding through a lack of financial resources. Desperate attempts were made by the partners to persuade leading factories, abroad as well as in Italy, to take on board their handiwork, but all were to prove fruitless. So the CNA organization

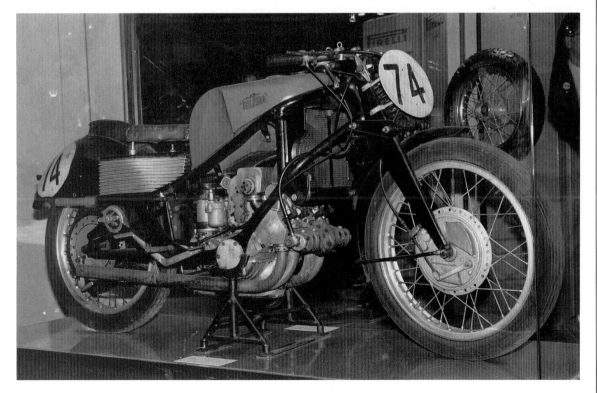

Swiss GP again, but three years on. A works mechanic is shown with the new aircooled model designed by Ing. Piero Remor. It was ridden into second spot in the 500 cc event on 3 July 1949 by Arciso Artesiani

(Compagnia Nazionale Aeronautica) of Rome, owned by Count Bonmartini, acquired the GRB assets and design. Ing. Gianini moved to CNA, but for a considerable time, he was involved purely in working on engines intended for light aircraft use.

It was not until 1934 that Count Bonmartini's enthusiasm for motorcycles found fresh expression in a redesigned version of the original four-cylinder machine. This was known as the Rondine (fast-flying Swallow). Ing. Remor once again became associated with Gianini in its development, and working with them was another engineer who was also a rider of considerable talent, Piero Taruffi.

The motorcycle they conceived had twin overhead camshafts (still with a central gear drive), inclined cylinders that were fully watercooled, and a supercharger. Power output was a sensational 86 bhp at 9000 rpm. Equipped with a four-speed gearbox with positive-stop foot-change, it was given a brilliant début at the Tripoli Autodrome, where Taruffi and Amilcare Rosetti scored an emphatic 1-2, beating the Guzzi and Norton factory teams.

The following year, with a partially-streamlined Rondine, Taruffi raised the 500 cc world records for the flying mile and kilometre to over 151.5 mph (244 kph). In that same year, however, Count Bonmartini sold his business to the vast Caproni aeronautical enterprise. However, as Caproni had no interest in two-wheelers at the time, it looked around for someone who would be interested in acquiring the Rondine portion of the CNA company.

This is where Giuseppe Gilera came on to the scene. Born into a working-class family, in a small village near Milan, in 1887, from an early age he had been fascinated by any form of mechanical transport. When only 15, the young Gilera entered employment with the Bianchi factory in Milan, where he gained his first practical experience.

Moving first to the Moto-Reve works and thence to the famous engineering firm of Bucher and Zeda, Giuseppe Gilera quickly built up a vast store of knowledge which was to serve him in good stead.

By now, the ambitious young engineer had also taken up road racing, and in particular gained recognition for his excellent showing in hillclimb events. However, the speed events always came second to his burning desire to become a motorcycle manufacturer in his own right. By 1909, at the age of 22, he was ready to take the plunge.

His first model was a 310 cc four-stroke single—an ohv engine with both inlet and exhaust valves operated mechanically, quite a rare layout at the time. Next came a V-twin and, thereafter, the first of the famous 500 cc ohv singles—forerunner of the ubiquitous post-World War 2 Saturno series, which made such a mark, not only on the road, but also in trials, motocross and road racing.

Right from the start, Giuseppe Gilera appreciated the importance of the publicity gained from sporting successes. Moto Gilera's first victory came at the Cremona circuit in 1912.

After World War 1, the demand for motorcycles accelerated rapidly, so Giuseppe Gilera decided to establish a new factory at Arcore, on the main road from Milan to Lecco. This was not far from Monza Park, where the famous autodrome was to be built.

Throughout the 1920s and early 1930s, Gilera not only grew into one of the country's largest factories, but gained considerable success in sporting events,

Above
The 1950 Gilera 500 cc World Champion, Umberto Masetti

Below
Remor (left) and Artesiani at the Italian GP in September 1949, before both left to join MV Agusta

such as trials and long-distance races. However, Gilera's ultimate aim was the international Grand Prix scene, and the chance to acquire the Rondine project, at the beginning of 1936, was heaven-sent.

Within a year, the machine had been completely updated as the result of a joint effort by Remor, Taruffi and Gilera himself. Its rigid, pressed-steel frame had been replaced by a tubular one incorporating swinging-arm rear suspension.

Under its new name and ownership, the revised supercharged four soon began to enjoy considerable success. For a short time in 1937 Taruffi became holder of the absolute world record, setting a speed of 170.15 mph for the flying kilometre, which just beat Britain's Eric Fernihough's 169.79 mph on a 995 cc Brough Superior JAP. However, it was almost immediately bettered by the 493 cc factory BMW of Ernst Henne, who set a new speed of 173.68 mph, although Taruffi's speed for the classic hour of 127 mph (205 kph) was to remain unbroken for many years.

In road racing, the most notable performance was Dorino Serafini's European Championship victory in

August 1939, during the Ulster GP (nominated that year as a championship event).

In 1940 the Gilera racing department employed the experience gained with the 500 cc machine as the basis for the development of an aircooled 250 cc four, which had its supercharger mounted in front of the crankcase instead of behind the cylinders. Although never actually raced, it was this smaller engine that set the pattern for the post-war 500 cc Gilera four.

Immediately after the war, the Arcore factory campaigned the old watercooled four but, although some reasonable results were gained in both solo and sidecar classes, the removal of the supercharger to conform with the FIM's newly-introduced ban on blowers saw the power drop by *half*, from 90 to 45 bhp. With virtually no saving in weight, the machine was no longer the competitive force it had once been, so an early decision was taken to construct a new version which would incorporate the design advances featured in the 1940 250.

Conceived by Ing. Remor, the new bike was ready by the end of 1947. Its aircooled engine, with the cylinders inclined 30 degrees forward from the vertical, produced 55 bhp at 8500 rpm. The four-speed gearbox was built in unit with the engine; and the

Below
The 1952-type 500 four which Masetti rode in the Swiss Grand Prix that year. Note the unusual tank

assembly mounted in a pressed-steel frame, which featured blade girder-type front forks with a central coil spring and torsion-bar swinging-arm rear suspension. The large-diameter alloy brake hubs were mounted in 20 in. diameter alloy wheel rims. Unlike the pre-war 500, the new design incorporated wet-sump lubrication. Carburation was taken care of by a new design of Weber instrument, one of which was fitted to each pair of cylinders. Magneto problems were solved by the adoption of a Marelli unit, mounted vertically behind the cylinder block. A wet multi-plate clutch was used, while the drive to the primary gears was taken from between the first and second cylinders.

Much attention had been taken in selecting the best, but at the same time lightest materials, which helped to provide Remor's creation with the surprisingly low weight of only 125 kg (275 lb), making it one of the lightest machines in its class at the time. Considering that the majority were single-cylinder designs, this was a notable achievement.

The bike was not raced until 1948, the initial test-

Alfredo Milani on his way to victory in the 1951 500 cc Italian GP at Monza. He averaged 105.19 mph for the 32-lap, 125-mile race

Overleaf
Eau Rouge, Belgian GP, 1952. Albino Milani keeps his Gilera outfit in front of Norton stars Cyril Smith (44) and Eric Oliver (2). Almost hidden from view is a second Gilera driven by Ernesto Merlo

ing having been carried out by Carlo Bandirola over the Milano-Bergamo *autostrada*. However, its race début, on 9 May at Cesena, was entrusted to the experienced Nello Pagani. If the gathered press, or indeed Gilera itself, had hoped for a successful first outing, those hopes were soon shattered. Quite simply, Pagani labelled the machine unrideable.

Although Massimo Masserini gave the new four its first victory in July, much of 1948 was spent in attempting to make the machine fully raceworthy. Besides its poor high-speed handling, the bike's main mechanical problem concerned its lubrication

system. To give some idea of how Pagani viewed the 1948 machine, it should be noted that he actually preferred to race his own 'private' single-cylinder Saturno.

Even so, Masserini won the important Italian GP, although his team-mate, Bandirola, blew up his four without a lap being completed.

The year 1949 signalled the introduction of the World Championship series. Masserini had retired, and the Gilera team now consisted of Pagani, Bandirola and new boy Arciso Artesiani.

With victories in Switzerland and Italy, Pagani finished the Grand Prix season in runner-up position, behind Leslie Graham (AJS), while the young Artesiani was third. The last proved a consistent finisher, with leader-board placings in all the races he contested, except for the Ulster, where a stone entered a carburettor, forcing his retirement.

At the end of that year, Ing. Remor, together with Artesiani and chief mechanic Arturo Magni, quit the Arcore team and joined its rival, MV Agusta.

Following Remor's departure, Giuseppe Gilera re-engaged Piero Taruffi as team manager. Instead of recruiting an outsider, Gilera promoted Remor's former assistants, Alessandro Columbo and Franco Passoni, to become joint heads of the technical department.

The new design team was obviously short on time to carry out any major changes prior to the start of the fast-approaching 1950 season, so it concentrated on the cylinder heads (there were now two, instead of a single casting), the carburettor size (which was upped to 30 mm with power rising to 52 bhp at

9000 rpm) and, perhaps of most importance, the lubrication system, which was greatly improved.

Another change following Remor's departure was that the rear springing reverted to the pre-war system, which consisted of horizontal cylindrical spring boxes at the base of the saddle, with friction damping. The braking system was also uprated by the fitment of a full-width front hub, but the blade girder forks were retained, even though the rival British factories were by now using the more modern telescopics.

As in earlier years, the Gilera riders, now with Umberto Masetti as a replacement for the departed Artesiani, gave the Isle of Man a miss. Then came two victories for Masetti in Holland and Belgium, with Pagani as runner-up on each occasion (although it should be remembered that both the AJS and Norton works teams were forced out through tyre trouble). Moreover, although Masetti could only

Above right
Pierre Monneret during his winning ride in the 500 cc French Grand Prix, May 1954. He also set the fastest lap at 114.07 mph

Right
Three important personalities of the 1954 Gilera race effort at the Senior TT that year. Left to right: Geoff Duke, Piero Taruffi and Giuseppe Gilera

Below
Gilera 500 four ridden in the 1954 French GP at Reims by race winner Pierre Monneret

finish sixth in Ulster, he came back to annex second behind race winner Duke (Norton) in the final round at Monza, taking the 1950 500 cc World Championship crown for the Arcore factory.

Although it had won the title, the Gilera team realized that it had been lucky, because the margin of victory had been a single point. If Duke had not struck problems in Holland and Belgium, the trophy would have been heading for the Norton headquarters in Birmingham, England.

The reason that the Norton had been so competitive was not its speed, but rather its excellent Featherbed frame and Roadholder telescopic forks. Thus, during the winter of 1950–1, Ing. Passoni undertook a total revision of the Gilera's running gear, using a round-tubed duplex frame with swinging-arm rear suspension and hydraulically-damped front forks of the Norton type. Additionally, smaller 19 in. rims and tyres, the latter of a wider profile, were specified.

The team for the 1951 season comprised Masetti, Pagani and Alfredo Milani. It should be noted that both Pagani and Milani often rode the Saturno singles during this period—even in the classics—rather than the four-cylinder model.

Besides the improvements outlined above, the fours had a much sleeker appearance, four instead of two carbs (in sizes ranging from 25 to 28 mm, depending on the circuit) and an additional 2 bhp in the engine department.

Bruno Francisci, Gilera's works rider in the 1955 Italian Senior Championship series, on his Arcore four

However, none of this was enough, with the result that Duke took both the 500 cc and 350 cc titles for Norton, becoming the first rider to achieve this feat in a single season. In the eight-round series, a Gilera did win on three occasions: Spain (Masetti), and France and Italy (Milani). At the last mentioned event, Gilera had scored a magnificent 1-2-3 (Milani, Masetti and Pagani) to dominate the event totally and issue a warning of future intentions to other teams.

A nose fairing had been tested at Monza, and this was incorporated into the 1952-type fours, while the tank was restyled and some other minor modifications carried out. However, after Duke put himself out of the running following a crash during a non-championship event at Schotten, Masetti took his and Gilera's second world crown, with wins at the Dutch TT and Belgian GP, plus second places at Monza and Barcelona.

Gilera's challenge in the sidecar class was dealt a great blow when its main contender for honours, Ercole Frigerio, was killed during the Swiss GP. Others who campaigned the fours in the sidecar class included Albino Milano (brother of Alfredo) and Ernesto Merlo.

For the 1953 season, team manager Piero Taruffi signed up Reg Armstrong and Dickie Dale, to be fol-

lowed later with the real scoop, Geoff Duke. They joined Masetti, Milani, Giuseppe Colnago and the Frenchman Pierre Monneret.

Following extensive testing at Monza, Ing. Passoni carried out a number of alterations suggested by the foreign riders, headed by Duke. These were to lead to the so-called 'Nortonized' model which, as the name suggests, had the appearance of a Norton. The engine, however, remained virtually the same.

For the first time, Gilera contested the Isle of Man TT, with Duke, Armstrong, Dale and Milani, but after Duke crashed, the best position gained was a third by Armstrong (who had won the same event in the previous year on a Norton). However, except in Ulster, Gilera riders and machines ruled supreme for the remainder of the classics, Duke taking the Championship, followed by Armstrong (second) and

Below
Gilera team bikes in the Monza paddock at the Italian GP, September 1955

Above
Following Geoff Duke's accident at Imola, at the beginning of 1957, Bob McIntyre was drafted into the squad. He was soon to repay this confidence with a dazzling display of skill in the Isle of Man

Overleaf
Isle of Man Senior TT, 1957, Bob McIntyre at Ginger Hall on his way to victory in the 500 cc event. He also won the 350 cc race, on an Arcore four, to score a memorable double

Duke (18) leads Alfredo Milani (6) over the line at the end of the 500 cc Italian GP, September 1957. They finished second and third, while another Gilera, ridden by Liberati, won the race

Milani (fourth). Meanwhile, Masetti had effectively quit the team at Assen, where he was involved in a dispute with team manager Taruffi following his accusation that the best machine had been given to Geoff Duke.

Although Gilera largely had things to itself, the team realized that the situation would not continue without further improvements, as Guzzi, Norton and, most notably, MV Agusta were carrying out their own development programmes in an attempt to wrest the world crown from the Arcore team.

By then Ing. Columbo had left, and development was solely in the hands of Ing. Passoni. It was he who instigated a major redesign for the 1954 season.

Particular effort was expended on the engine. For a start, the 58 mm stroke was lengthened to 58.8 mm, giving a new capacity of 499.504 cc. The sump was redesigned to allow the engine to be mounted lower in the frame, yet at the same time ground clearance was increased by tucking the exhaust pipes closer to the engine. The valve angle was widened from 80 to 90 degrees (eventually to 100 degrees), while the valve diameter was also changed. The exhaust valves, which were sodium cooled, were 15 per cent smaller in diameter than the inlet valves. All eight valves had helical springs, enclosed by cylindrical tappets which were in direct contact with the cams.

Various types of crankshaft were tried: a forged one-piece item, necessitating the use of split big-ends and split cages for the big-end rollers; a built-up version in several pieces that were pressed together; and a built-up type assembled by the Hirth process. Some were constructed by Gilera itself, while others were made by a specialist German company. Built-up crankshafts were ultimately found to provide the best results, having a life of between 50 and 100 hours under racing conditions. A total of six main bearings supported the crankshaft, and the whole engine/gearbox unit benefited from the wide use of bearings and bushes of more than adequate capacity. The gearbox itself acquired a fifth ratio, mainly to provide a lower first gear, and thus restrict the use of the clutch.

Experiments were carried out with coil/battery ignition, but it was found that the latest type of Lucas rotating-magnet magneto provided the best results. Power output was a claimed 64 bhp at 10,500 rpm.

Changes to the cycle parts were limited to shortening the frame, narrowing the rear forks, fitting a

Above
Romolo Ferri in action at Monza on the 125 twin, during the famous record-breaking session staged by Gilera after quitting GP racing in November 1957

Left
Inside the Gilera 125 twin record-breaking machine, Monza, 13 November 1957

streamlined cowling and introducing a more powerful (and larger diameter) twin-leading-shoe front stopper.

On the riding side, Dale and Pagani had been poached by MV Agusta, leaving Duke, Armstrong and Masetti, plus new boy Libero Liberati, who mainly raced in Italy that year. In addition, Frenchman Pierre Monneret continued to be loaned a machine on occasion. With this line-up, Gilera dominated the proceedings at all but three of the Championship events to take the title.

Officially, there were nine rounds, but the 1954 500 cc Championship was reduced to only eight that counted towards the points table, after the Ulster GP had its race distance reduced below the FIM minimum due to bad weather.

Monneret got the season under way by winning on home soil at Reims. Then Duke proceeded to win five rounds in a row, with wins in Belgium, Holland,

Germany, Switzerland and Italy. He carried off his fifth title by a clear 20 points from his nearest challenger, the Norton ace, Ray Amm.

At Monza, in September, Gilera tried a full-enclosure, streamlined 'dustbin' shell for the first time. It was a foretaste of things to come.

For 1955 the four-cylinder Gilera remained virtually unaltered, except for a large cooling scoop for the front brake—and the adoption of the enclosed streamlining for all of the team bikes. However, some riders openly voiced the opinion that this was not a welcome addition.

The seasonal game of 'musical chairs' played by riders and manufacturers, saw Masetti leave to join MV Agusta. Thus, the 1955 Gilera squad consisted of Duke, Armstrong, Liberati, Colnago and Milani, plus occasionally Monneret, Martin (Belgium) and Veer (Holland).

It was to be Duke's last great year, he was suspended (together with Armstrong) by the FIM following the 1955 Dutch TT. Then a serious accident at Imola, before the 1957 classic season had even got under way, effectively strangled the career of this truly great rider.

However, by taking the 1955 500 cc title, Duke had clearly established himself as not only capable of winning the 'Blue Riband' event for three consecutive seasons aboard the Arcore four-cylinder model, but also as a true ambassador for the sport.

Armstrong finished the year in runner-up spot, while fellow Gilera teamster, Colnago, came fourth.

One mechanical problem that year had been a spate of broken valve springs, later traced to faulty heat treatment.

At the tail-end of the season, Duke raced a factory Gilera four at a quartet of English short circuits—at Silverstone and Brands Hatch, he was beaten by a certain youngster named John Surtees, aboard a single-cylinder Norton. In the following year, this was to lead to Gilera facing its first serious challenge for several seasons, when that man Surtees was mounted on the rival four-cylinder MV Agusta in the World Championship.

The end of 1955 had also seen another significant change—Piero Taruffi quit as team manager to concentrate upon his four-wheel activities. He was

Former Gilera works rider and 1957 500 cc World Champion, Libero Liberati, pictured with his 'private' single-cylinder Saturno model at the Vallelunga circuit near Rome, October 1961. Early the following year, while riding the same machine, he was killed in a road accident near his Terni home

The notional third wheel of Albino Milani's 500 cc Gilera four-cylinder 'sidecar' record-breaker

replaced by the next generation of Gilera, the young and very enthusiastic Ferruccio.

The FIM ban meant that Gilera was without both Duke and Armstrong for the first two rounds of the 1956 season (the Isle of Man TT and the Dutch TT). That year the Championship consisted of only six events that counted towards the 500 cc world title. Therefore, the Arcore team was at a great disadvantage, particularly after its main challenger, MV, scored two victories, thanks to new boy Surtees.

Ing. Passoni had carried out further modifications during the closed season. These saw the frame strengthened considerably, a new 'dustbin' fairing with greatly improved aerodynamics, an exhaust system which now included four megaphones, and an improvement in power to 70 bhp at 11,000 rpm. These changes also added considerably to the machine's weight, which had risen to 150 kg (330 lb).

The third round in the series saw Duke make the headlines—'Still the Master! Geoff Duke (Gilera) builds up a one-minute lead on John Surtees (MV Agusta) in 500 cc class of Belgian Grand Prix and then retires in the closing stages', was a typical caption. This victory meant that Surtees had effectively won the title, even though he fell during the next round at Solitude, putting himself out for the rest of the season with a fractured left arm.

Duke's retirement in the Belgian GP had been caused by a shattered piston, which Gilera put down to poor quality fuel.

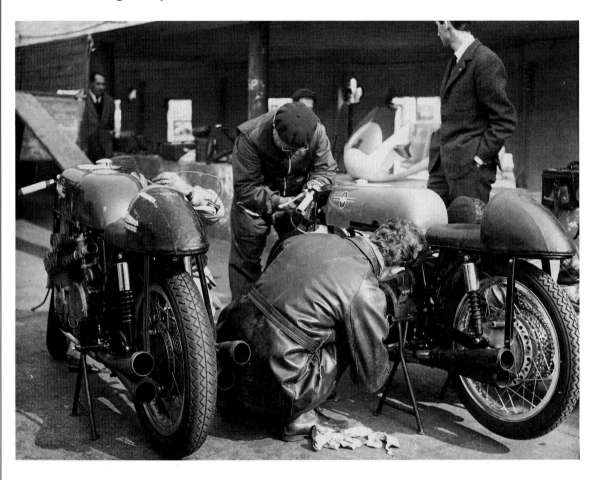

Gilera returned to racing in March 1963 through the Duke Scuderia team. Here mechanics prepare one of the 1957 350 fours during testing at Monza

The only real consolation, for what had been a less-than-happy year, came in the final round at Monza, where not only did Gilera take the first four places in the 500 cc race (Duke, Liberati, Monneret and Armstrong), but the company also débuted a new 349.66 cc (46 × 52.6 mm) version of its four-cylinder design. With either 22 or 25 mm Dell'Ortos, depending upon the circuit, the engine produced 49 bhp at 11,000 rpm. Two of the smaller Gileras appeared on the start line, and although Duke retired, Liberati kept going for the whole race distance to win comfortably from Dickie Dale's Guzzi. The main problem, which the smaller-capacity four carried throughout its career, was excess weight. Being a sleeved-down 500 cc machine, it could never expect to provide as strong a challenge as its older brother could in the 'Blue Riband' class.

Not only had Ing. Passoni been working on the smaller four, but also a brand-new 125 twin, which appeared at Monza in May, with lightweight special-ist Romolo Ferri at the helm. Its start-to-finish victory over a pack of MVs and Mondials had created great interest, but the Grand Prix career of this interesting 124.656 cc (40 × 49.6 mm) machine was destined to be blighted by mechanical gremlins. It was to score only a solitary classic victory, when Ferri won the 1956 German Grand Prix.

The year was brought to a close by two off-circuit incidents which were to have a significant effect on Gilera's competition activities, but in vastly different ways. In September, after racing at the Avus circuit in Berlin, Armstrong announced his retirement; in the following month, Ferruccio Gilera succumbed to a heart attack while visiting the company's Argentinian subsidiary in Buenos Aires.

The first incident was to lead to the Scot Bob McIntyre joining the team, while Ferruccio's untimely death not only robbed the team of a most enthusiastic member (he had largely been responsible for Passoni designing the new 125 twin and 350 four-cylinder models), but it also drained Giuseppe Gilera of the determination and drive which had created what was, at that time, one of the truly great racing teams in the world. It was almost as if he had lost much of the will even to live, so great was the loss of his only son.

And so to 1957, destined to be a year of drama. First, as related earlier, Duke put himself out of action after casting the plot away in spectacular fashion at the Imola Gold Cup season's opener. At the same meeting, McIntyre's machine was sidelined after electrical problems set in. In the classics, Liberati scored a double at Hockenheim, after McIntyre struck problems in both races. However, the Scot roared back to score one of the most famous double victories of all time, when he won the Junior and Senior Golden Jubilee TTs—the latter staged over *eight* laps (302 miles!) of the legendary 37¾-mile mountain circuit. McIntyre also became the first rider to lap the famous circuit in excess of 100 mph. In addition, Aussie Bob Brown was drafted into the team for the Isle of Man, scoring a pair of fine third places.

McIntyre suffered an accident in Holland, the consequence being a neck injury that was to afflict him for the remainder of the season. Even though

The Scuderia équipe at the 1963 IoM TT. Left to right: John Hartle, Geoff Duke and Phil Read (the last had been brought into the team following Derek Minter's Brands Hatch crash in the previous month)

he and Duke were fit enough to ride in the final two rounds (in Ulster and Italy), it allowed Liberati to become the top Gilera points scorer in both the 350 cc and 500 cc categories, resulting in him being the runner-up and Champion in those events respectively.

Virtually no changes had been made to the Gileras from the 1956 models, this being a sign that all was not well within the camp. The vital spark seemed to be missing during the 1957 season, although that probably went unnoticed at the time.

When the chance came to withdraw after almost 50 years of competitive motorcycle sport, Giuseppe Gilera grabbed it with both hands. It took the form of a tripartite agreement between Guzzi, Mondial and Gilera, all of whom announced their withdrawal from Grand Prix racing at the end of the year. For Guzzi and Mondial, the reason was purely financial, but for Giuseppe Gilera it was also the depression caused by his son's death.

Before finally mothballing its racing bikes, Gilera went on a records spree at Monza, during which Bob McIntyre set a new speed record of 141 mph for the coveted hour title on a *350 cc* four. Albino Milani also established a new world sidecar record of 116 mph.

Then there followed a period of over four years

The 500 Gilera four, as it appeared in 1963

when rumours were rife about the marque's intentions of making a Grand Prix comeback. The truth was that no such comeback had been contemplated during this time, even though countless riders and sponsors had plagued the Gilera camp with their pleas.

In August 1962 the former Gilera star, Bob McIntyre, crashed his 500 cc Norton at Oulton Park and was fatally injured. A remembrance meeting was staged at the same circuit a few weeks later, and as a mark of respect, the Arcore factory staff sent one of the 'dustbin'-faired fours over for Geoff Duke to parade around the circuit. It was this event which was to trigger a Gilera comeback.

In early March 1963 came the news that the famous Arcore fours would race again, under the 'private' Scuderia Duke banner, with Derek Minter and John Hartle as riders. Their first race would be on 6 April at Silverstone.

I was there that day and can still recall the expectant tension which everyone in the crowd felt. Although Minter won the race, the sight of Norton-mounted Phil Read splitting the Italian fours, on what was, after all, a speed circuit, made one realize that Gilera might not do as well as everyone had thought.

And so it transpired. First Minter was badly injured before the classics even got under way, after an accident on one of his Norton singles at Brands Hatch in May. Then Read was brought into the squad as a replacement. At the first Grand Prix, at Hockenheim, the smaller four was totally outclassed for speed, not just by the full-works Honda fours

and Bianchi twins, but also by the pre-production Honda CR77 *twin*. Even though Hartle brought a 350 Gilera home second in the Junior TT, the writing was clearly on the wall and they were soon withdrawn so that the team could 'concentrate on the 500 cc class'.

However, although more competitive, except at an early non-championship event at Imola, the bigger Gileras simply could not match the lone MV Agusta of Mike Hailwood. Hartle gave the Scuderia Duke équipe its only classic victory when he won the Dutch TT, but this was due to Hailwood's MV blowing up on the second lap of the race.

Minter had returned to the team by August, but this did not seem to make any real improvement in Gilera's fortunes.

Then came a period of uncertainty as to whether or not the company would race in 1964. It carried out more testing at Monza—this time with several Italian riders, such as Renzo Rossi, Franco Mancini and Gilberto Milani. John Hartle was also there, riding one of the fours equipped with British Reynolds leading-link front forks. Still no official statement was made one way or the other.

The first round of the 1964 World Championship was held at Daytona, Florida, the 500 cc race taking place on 2 February. This created something of a stir when, for some 75 miles, Mike Hailwood, then the undisputed master of the sport, fought tooth and nail

Instrument and control layout of the 500 Gilera four

The US Grand Prix at Daytona, in March 1964, saw a titanic battle between Benedicto Caldarella (Gilera, 6) and Mike Hailwood (MV, 1) during the early stages of the race

to overcome the little-known Argentinian Benedicto Caldarella. The champion was on his MV, the challenger on a Gilera. Only gearbox trouble finally removed Caldarella from this amazing battle. For lap after lap of the 3.1-mile giant speedbowl, the two Italian fours were involved in the closest 500 cc battle for years. It later transpired that the Gilera was one of the Scuderia Duke bikes which had been sent to the Argentine at the end of 1963.

As if to prove that the United States GP was no fluke, Caldarella won the 500 cc class at the Imola meeting in April at record speed (Hailwood was not there).

Gilera had also loaned the Swiss sidecar star Florian Camathias an engine for record-breaking purposes and 'selected' World Championship meetings at the beginning of 1964. After Camathias won the opening classic in Spain, observers believed that Gilera would mount a serious challenge for both solo and three-wheel honours that season, but a series of strikes and other problems at the Arcore factory effectively ruined all chances of success for both Caldarella and Camathias. The result was that the

only other World Championship success came in the final round at Monza, where the diminutive Argentinian finished second to Hailwood. He was some 10 seconds down, but was credited with the fastest lap at 121.08 mph.

The strikes had intensified the financial decline of the once great marque and meant that any hope of Gilera competing in 1965 had to be forgotten. However, the Italian race organizers made vast offers of financial assistance to Gilera (and Guzzi) as an encouragement to reappear in 1966. This 'pot of gold' induced Gilera to come out of retirement.

The much-travelled Ing. Lino Tonti was consulted in an attempt to make the ageing machines more competitive; he proposed a small number of changes, the most significant being a new, slimmer fairing and, more importantly perhaps, a six-speed (and later seven-speed) gearbox. In addition, the duplex front brake, first tested in 1957, was re-introduced.

In what was clearly something of a second-rate effort, riders Remo Venturi and Derek Minter did the best they could. However, a series of mechanical problems and a crash by Minter during TT practice conspired to blunt the challenge even further.

The final appearances of the 500 cc four-cylinder Gileras came in October. The first was at Brands Hatch, where Venturi and ex-Suzuki teamster Frank

Left

Caldarella during his Italian visit, summer 1964. Sadly, he was hampered by a strike-bound factory and lack of finance in his bid for glory

Right

Remo Venturi with a model of the 500 cc Gilera from the Protar series manufactured by ex-racer Tarquinio Provini, who had been forced to quit the sport in 1966 after crashing while practising for the TT

Perris could only finish mid-field, while the final sortie was at Vallelunga, just north of Rome. Venturi finished runner-up to Pasolini's Benelli, after Agostini's MV had retired.

Although both Minter and Perris tried to obtain bikes for the 1967 season, Giuseppe Gilera finally called it a day. He had realized that one of the greatest racing motorcyles of all time had finally come to the end of the road.

A few short months later, at the end of 1968, the Gilera company was forced to appoint a receiver. Early in the following year, the giant Piaggio concern took over, and although it survives to this day, Gilera has never been allowed a Grand Prix comeback.

Below

Remo Venturi giving the Gilera its last foreign outing at Brands Hatch, 9 October 1966. Another Gilera was also ridden at the same meeting by Frank Perris. Both finished in mid-field positions—a sad end to a glorious racing history

6

Guzzi

Today 'Moto' Guzzi's production is centred around its line of 90-degree V-twins. All of these are viewed by their owners and the press alike as offering basic and traditional values, rather than an up-to-the-minute, glitzy, hi-tech image. This is all a far cry from some of the highly-innovative and trend-setting Guzzi machinery of the past . . . take the first ever Guzzi motorcycle, for example, which appeared in 1919.

This prototype—which carried the motif GP (Guzzi-Parodi) on its tank—was conceived during World War 1 by Carlo Guzzi, mechanic and friend of two fighter pilots, Giovanni Ravelli and Giorgio Parodi. The trio were ardent motorcycle enthusiasts who decided that they would pool their talents and resources, after the war, to create a company to

The 1946 Guzzi 494.8 cc (68 × 68 mm), 120-degree V-twin was a development of Stanley Woods' 1935 Senior TT winner

manufacture Guzzi's brainchild. Unfortunately, Ravelli was killed in a flying accident during the last days of the conflict, but Guzzi and Parodi survived to carry through the dream and, soon after the termination of hostilities, the pair readied their sensational prototype machine.

Unorthodox features abounded, many of them being taken directly from aeronautical engineering practice, which had accelerated sharply during the latter stages of the war. This first ever Guzzi featured a horizontal cylinder for improved cooling and greater stability from its lower centre of gravity. The engine's bore and stroke dimensions were over-square at 88 × 82 mm, providing a lower piston speed and greater volumetric efficiency. The four inclined valves also contributed to much superior breathing. They were operated by a single overhead camshaft, driven by a shaft and bevel gear at the offside of the cylinder. A positive gear-type oil pump was driven from the nearside end of the cam-

This interesting 250 cc dohc twin appeared in 1948. Designed by Ing. Antonio Micucci, it offered real potential—but the Guzzi management chose to concentrate upon the old-fashioned flat-single in the quarter-litre category

shaft. An external flywheel, also on the nearside, offered not only extra balance, but allowed the use of a much smaller crankcase. Ignition was by a magneto mounted atop the engine.

Maximum power output of the 1919 prototype 498.4 cc engine was 17 bhp, which provided a road speed of around 80 mph; outstanding figures for a single-cylinder 500 of 1919. In fact, Carlo Guzzi's creation was of extremely advanced concept for its time—sohc, oversquare dimensions, four valves per cylinder, unit construction and geared primary drive. This has to be seen against its typical contempories—side-valve, long-stroke, two valves per cylinder, separate engine/gearbox/clutch, and chain or belt primary drive.

Ultimately, by the time commercial production (under the Guzzi name) began in 1921, some of these features had been replaced by less advanced and *cheaper* alternatives. However, Carlo Guzzi had shown himself to be a forward-thinking engineer of the highest order. This ability was to be demonstrated time and time again through the years, until the

company's founding fathers, Parodi and Guzzi, passed on—the former from a heart attack in 1955, and the latter in 1965, worn out from years of creative work.

In fact, the Mandello del Lario factory's engineers came up with a whole host of racing designs: myriad flat singles, a parallel twin, an across-the-frame three-cylinder, a wide-angle V-twin, a watercooled inline four and, finally, perhaps the most exotic motorcycle of all time, the legendary watercooled V8. Because of this, Guzzi machinery was rarely out of the headlines between the marque's first classic victory (the 1924 German GP) and the outbreak of World War 2. After the end of hostilities, the bikes soon resumed their winning ways, and in 1947 Guzzi machinery won 60 foreign races and 205 Italian races. Guzzi also captured the 250 and 500 cc Senior Italian Championships, the former by Dario Ambrosini (later to join Benelli), and the latter by the veteran Omobono Tenni.

My earlier book *Moto Guzzi Singles* (Osprey) covered the racing career of the various horizontal 'one-lungers', so rather than repeat this and, in the process, provide nothing more than a thumb-nail sketch of all of Guzzi's classic racers, I have decided to concentrate on three of the most interesting, if not perhaps the most successful of these varied designs. These are the late 1940s parallel twin, the early 1950s inline four, and the breathtaking V8.

Above
*The Mandello concern made a grave error of
judgement in not proceeding with the innovative 250
twin designed by Micucci. The original 1947 prototype
is shown here*

Right
*One of Italy's most underrated riders, Enrico
Lorenzetti, at the 1948 Ulster GP with his works
246.8 cc Gambalunghino*

Below
*The definitive version of the dohc 250, as raced by
Manliff Barrington in the 1948 Lightweight TT.
Compare this with the prototype*

250 parallel twin

The quarter-litre *Bicilindrica Bialbero* (twin-cylinder, double-camshaft) project was the responsibility of Ing. Antonio Micucci, who joined Guzzi in the winter of 1942 and became managing designer in 1945. It was in September that year that Carlo Guzzi laid out the basic specification for the machine, which Ing. Micucci subsequently proceeded to bring to life. Progress was rapid, for very early in 1946, construction of the prototype began. Less than a year later, the machine was ready to undergo its first tests.

The original design had been for a supercharged machine, so the heads of the 247.2 cc (54 × 54 mm) dohc twin had been laid out with valves inclined at 60 degrees. The change to a normally-aspirated engine, necessitated by the FIM's ban on superchargers, entailed major modifications. The most important of these was a new design of head with the valve guides at 80 degrees to accommodate larger-diameter valves. At a very early stage in the engine's development, the power was superior to that being achieved by the existing single-cylinder Albatros racer. These tests were not only carried out on the bench, but also on the *autostrada*, where the new twin proved itself capable of close to 100 mph first time out. This equated to a shade over 20 bhp

The 1949 250 cc Ulster Grand Prix winner, Englishman Maurice Cann

at 9100 rpm; all this on low-grade, 73-octane fuel. Ultimately, the power output was raised to 25 bhp, with the engine revolutions trimmed back to 9000. Correspondingly, maximum speed went up to around the 105 mph mark.

The double-knocker parallel twin engine had its cylinders facing forward at an angle of 30 degrees to the horizontal. Hiduminium was employed for both the cylinder barrels and heads. The former were cast as one, but featured a hair-line cut between the cylinder bases. Bronze hemispheres, cast in, formed the combustion chambers. The crankcase and gearbox housing were manufactured in electron. The crankshaft was supported by three main bearings and had bolted-on bobweights on the two middle cheeks; the central bearing was of the needle-roller type. On the timing side of the crankshaft there was a ball bearing, which located the shaft, and on the drive side a roller bearing, which accommodated lateral movement caused by expansion of the crankcase. Both timing and drive shafts were of 30 mm diameter; the crankpins 23 mm. On the drive side shaft there was an outside flywheel with a diameter of 190 mm and a thickness of 16 mm. Drive to the twin camshafts was by gears.

A double gear-type oil pump was located within the camshaft drive cover, while there was a return pump, with gauze filter, below the crankshaft. Lubricant was fed from the 4.5-litre (1-gallon) oil tank, which was mounted in rubber beneath the saddle. The big-ends were supplied at a rate of just over 180 litres (40 gallons) per hour, and the camshafts at 126 litres (28 gallons) per hour.

The valves featured shim-set adjustment and had head diameters of 23 mm (exhaust) and 29 mm (inlet). The bronze valve guides were unusual, featuring abnormally large external dimensions and being tapered on the outside to mate with similar tapers in the cylinder heads. On the outer portion, there was a circular groove, which formed a bearing surface for balls that carried and centralized the valve spring assembly. This was of the coil variety, there being two per valve—the 250 single of the period employed hairpins.

Other technical details included a pair of 26 mm Dell'Orto carburettors with a single, remotely-mounted float chamber, a German Bosch magneto, geared primary drive, four-speed close-ratio gear-box (the gears could be removed without stripping the engine), a 14-plate clutch and 21 in. wheels. The machine had a dry weight of 116 kg (266 lb).

The original prototype, with which all the test programme was carried out, was joined by a second machine in the spring of 1948.

At the end of May, company president, Giorgio Parodi, together with Ing. Micucci, Omobono Tenni, Ing. Moretto (engine specialist), two mechanics and a total of ten Guzzi motorcycles arrived in the Isle of Man for the forthcoming TT. Included were the two 250 cc twins. Both were for Stanley Woods' protégé, Dubliner Manliff Barrington, to ride.

After completing a relatively trouble-free practice period, Barrington's twin led the Lightweight race for the first two laps, but on lap 3, the Irishman's luck ran out when the twin gave up the ghost near Kirkmichael village. Before his retirement, Barrington had averaged around 75 mph. *The Motor Cycle* commented: 'It (the 250 twin) is too new for immediate triumph, but will be hard to lick in 1949!'

Sadly, this was not to be, for Guzzi decided to update the venerable single instead, shelving any future development of the twin. In the light of subsequent events, this was to prove a shortsighted move, as the appearance of the twin-cylinder NSU Rennmax in 1952 halted Moto Guzzi's dominance in the quarter-litre class. It is my considered opinion that had Guzzi continued with Micucci's twin, the Mandello factory would have been in a much more favourable position to respond to the German challenge when it came . . . but, of course, I can make that statement with the benefit of hindsight, something the Guzzi management did not have.

By 1950 the venerable 120-degree V-twin looked like this. It was finally pensioned off in the following year

Left
Dual-carb, four-valve dohc single engine, circa 1952

Right
Lorenzetti at the Ospendaletti circuit, during testing of the new 500 inline four-cylinder model, February 1953

Below
The prototype single-carb, two-valve motor, February 1953

Overleaf
Generally, the inline four was a grave disappointment to the Mandello factory. Here Fergus Anderson (87) finishes mid-field at the Blandford international meeting on 3 August 1953

500 inline four

Giorgio Parodi was the man who instigated a series of events which were to lead to one of Guzzi's most unusual designs, the 500 inline four. Parodi had seen his factory's existing 500 V-twin effectively out-classed in 1950 by not only the new Featherbed-framed, single-cylinder Norton, but also by the emerging four-cylinder models from both Gilera and MV Agusta. So, in 1951, he commissioned the Rome-based engineer, Ing. Carlo Gianni, to come up with a rival four-cylinder design.

Together with Piero Remor (and later Piero Taruffi), Gianni had been largely responsible for the forerunner, of the Gilera, the supercharged, four-cylinder OPRA and Rondine models.

Both Parodi and Gianni felt that an across-the-frame four was a non-starter, for two reasons. One was that both the Guzzi factory and Ing. Gianni would be accused of simply copying existing designs, the other was that the inline layout would provide the same frontal area as Guzzi's existing singles and V-twins, but with the addition of more power.

Shaft-drive and rear hub details of the ill-fated 500 Guzzi inline four

Anderson débuted a revised version of the inline four at Monza in September 1953. Besides the streamlining, several modifications had been carried out in an attempt to improve the roadholding and handling qualities

Unfortunately, there were also two major problems with the design; torque reaction from the shaft drive put it at a disadvantage on twisty circuits, while the engine-speed clutch made it virtually impossible to guarantee precise cog swapping at racing speeds. It is also probably true to say that had fairings been in widescale use, the Gianni engine would not have been contemplated; the full 'dustbin' streamlining, which was to become an almost standard feature of Italian racing bikes by the mid 1950s, ensured that the across-the-frame fours were not penalized so much for their increased frontal area.

In many ways, the Gianni engine followed aeronautical, rather than motorcycle, engineering practice, looking very similar to designs such as the Daimler Benz DB601 and Rolls Royce Merlin (which powered the Messerschmitt Bf109 and Supermarine Spitfire aircraft respectively).

The inline four featured two valves per cylinder, spur-gear drive for the twin overhead camshafts, watercooling, magneto ignition, a gearbox in unit with the engine, and shaft final drive. Distinctly unorthodox for a motorcycle unit at the time was the fuel system, a full description of which follows later. The dimensions were oversquare, with a bore of 56 mm and a stroke of 50 mm, giving a cylinder capacity of 492.2 cc.

The 1954 Guzzi 500 inline four with fully-streamlined 'dustbin' fairing. Note the large air vent near the top of the fairing

Another interesting feature of the engine was the use of a built-up crankshaft with one-piece connecting rods and Hirth couplings. The crankshaft was supported by a total of five bearings: a ball bearing at the rear, a double-row roller in the middle, and three single-row roller bearings. The connecting rods were steel forgings with phosphor-bronze small-ends and single-row, roller-bearing big-ends.

Each high-dome forged piston had an 11:1 compression ratio and carried two compression rings. Below the gudgeon-pin bosses was a slotted oil-scraper ring.

A one-piece aluminium-alloy casting formed the upper half of the crankcase, the cylinder block and the cylinder head. Cast-iron wet liners were screwed into position. The lower half of the crankcase was retained by nuts on long studs extending down into the main casting. Oil was contained in an integral sump at the base of the lower crankcase, there being 4.5 litres (1 gallon) of lubricant, which was distributed around the engine assembly by a gear-type pump.

The valves had head diameters of 30 mm (exhaust) and 32 mm (inlet); shim caps were used to obtain the correct valve clearances. Like the 250 twin, coil springs were used. The valves themselves were seated directly into the cylinder head (a feature also employed on the 1960s Bianchi dohc twins—see Chapter 3).

Water was circulated around the engine and the forward-mounted radiator by thermo-syphon action, assisted by an impeller bolted to the front of the cylinder block. This was driven by spur gears from the crankshaft.

The single-spring clutch had four bonded friction plates and a matching number of steel plates, while the gearbox was a four-speeder. Within the gearbox casing was the bevel drive to the vertically-mounted Marelli magneto.

Without doubt, the design's most interesting feature was its fuel system. Essentially, this was of the forced-atomization type, whereby a Roots-type blower supplied air to the valves, which were opened by cams on the inlet camshaft. Fuel was fed by a pump to the jets, from which it reached the engine, while surplus fuel was returned to the tanks. These were of the pannier, gravity type and had a capacity of 28 litres (6 gallons).

With a dry weight of 145 kg (320 lb) and maximum power of 54 bhp at 9000 rpm, the 500 inline four was capable of over 140 mph. Even though it suffered a mechanical failure during its racing début at Siracusa, early in 1953, the design seemed vindicated when, in the following month of May, Enrico Lorenzetti won the 500 cc race at an international meeting over the super-fast Hockenheim circuit in Germany. At the same event, Fergus Anderson had set the fastest lap at 113 mph on a sister machine.

After this, however, except for an all too brief spell in the Italian GP at Monza before it retired, the inline four failed to deliver the goods by way of consistent race results. Not only did it prove less than reliable, but it was hampered by its torque reaction and poor handling over the short, twistier circuits.

Again in 1954, after a winning start to the season at Mettet, in Belgium, the four failed to live up to expectations. Thus it was replaced, first by a new single and subsequently by the ultimate Guzzi racer, the V8.

500 V8

The most well known and respected of all Moto Guzzi's racing technicians is, without doubt, Ing. Giulio Cesare Carcano. It was Carcano who created the range of Guzzi singles which dominated the 350 cc World Championship during a five-year period between 1953 and 1957, and it was he who

Leading Guzzi privateer Arthur Wheeler during his winning, but wet, ride in one of the 250 cc races at Silverstone's Hutchinson 100 meeting, August 1954

designed the world's only eight-cylinder Grand Prix motorcycle.

This unique racer came about because the single-cylinder model was not quick enough against the 500 four-cylinder Gileras and MVs, and because the inline four was not able to stay with the opposition on any but the faster circuits. Finally, after watching the Italian GP at Monza, in September 1954, Carcano decided to develop an entirely new design.

At first, Carcano considered a six-cylinder layout, but soon plumped for an eight. In the latter, the cylinders were arranged in two blocks of four, at an angle of 90 degrees. The axis of the engine was laid across the frame to simplify the employment of chain final drive, which Carcano considered absolutely vital after his experience with the ill-fated inline four.

The reason for the complex design? Cubic capacity of each cylinder could be reduced to a minimum

Above

Dutch TT, 1954. Factory rider Alano Montanari managed to finish sixth in the 350 cc race, despite a fall which damaged his bike's fairing

Below

Ken Kavanagh (left) and Ing. Carcano, after the former had won the 1956 Junior TT

to give very high rpm and consequent high power output. There was the added attraction that the originality of the design gave great possibilities of development, while the overall dimensions, both longitudinal and transversal, could still be quite reasonable, enabling the engine unit to be housed in a conventional, double-cradle frame.

The project crystallized during the winter of 1954–5, in an atmosphere of the greatest secrecy. However, Ing. Carcano was not only a brilliant designer, and a champion yachtsman, but he also had a great sense of humour. As a vivid illustration of this, without adding any written explanation, he sent his friends in the press, who were clamouring for information, a drawing of his latest project, seen only from the offside. He invited them to guess what it was, but not one journalist came up with the correct answer—one even went as far as suggesting that it was a turbine-powered device!

Specially-prepared 350 Guzzi sidecar outfit, with which a number of factory riders annexed 25 world speed records at Montlhéry on 1 November 1955

The Carcano masterpiece first appeared in public mid-way through 1955, at an Italian national meeting at Senigallia. The newcomer caused a great stir in racing circles throughout the world, even though it was not raced that day. The same thing happened at its second appearance, during practice for the Italian Grand Prix at Monza later that year. Finally, its actual race début came at Imola on Easter Monday 1956, when Guzzi works rider Ken Kavanagh completed ten laps before retiring in the 500 cc Gold Cup Race.

With bore and stroke dimensions of 44 × 42 mm, giving each cylinder a swept volume of 62.31 cc, the 498.58 cc engine was very slightly oversquare, with a 0.932:1 bore-to-stroke ratio. During the early stages of its development, power output of the V8 was in the region of 65 bhp at 12,000 rpm, but gradually this figure was increased. By the end of 1957, when unfortunately Guzzi decided to withdraw from Grand Prix racing, it had been boosted to nearly 80 bhp at 14,000 rpm—almost 10 bhp more than the most potent rival 500 fours, and unsurpassed until the 1970s.

A point worth mentioning is the fact that even at 14,000 rpm, the linear speed of the tiny pistons was actually *lower* than that of a typical 500 cc single-cylinder racing engine of the period, such as a Manx Norton or Gilera Saturno, turning over at 7000 rpm.

Owing to its cylinder arrangement, the V8 engine needed watercooling, the radiator being situated ahead of the crankcase. The water pump was driven by one of a train of six timing gears (housed in an oil bath on the offside of the engine), which operated the twin overhead camshafts for each bank of cylinders.

On the nearside of each inlet camshaft was a pair of distributors, each with four contact-breakers. The coils, one for each cylinder, were mounted in two clusters of four on each side of the frame's front down-tubes. Dual 6-volt batteries were housed on each side of the rear frame section, and the firing order was 1-8-3-6-4-5-2-7. To provide more space for the two valves per cylinder in their hemispherical combustion chambers, 10 mm sparking plugs were specified.

The short, massive, forged nickel-chrome crankshaft, with circular flywheels, was supported by a total of five caged-roller bearings, with split races between each throw. Split roller bearings were also used for the big-ends of the 90 mm long connecting rods. The crankcase was a truly superb one-piece casting in electron, while the cast-iron wet-liner cylinders were finned at the top, within the water jacket, for more efficient cooling.

The valves, operating in split guides, were set at an angle of 58 degrees to each other, their diameters being 21 mm for the exhaust, and 23 mm for the inlet. Each had dual coil springs, over which large tappets came into direct contact with the cams. The highly-domed forged pistons, deeply recessed for valve clearance and also to provide a squish effect, carried two compression rings and a single oil-scraper ring. Following conventional Guzzi racing practice (unlike the Gianni-designed inline four), the lubrication system was of the dry-sump variety, the oil pump being gear driven at half engine speed. The oil tank itself was in the large-diameter top frame tube and had a capacity of 5 litres (just over a gallon).

Each miniature cylinder was fed by its own 20 mm Dell'Orto carburettor, there being two float chambers on the nearside of the power unit, each serving four instruments. A single cable from the quick-action twistgrip operated the eight throttle slides with an extremely efficient linkage system, which reduced effort to a bare minimum.

There was a dry clutch, while the geared primary drive ran in an oil-bath casing and provided an engine-to-gearbox ratio of 2.75:1. Amazingly, there

This and the following two photographs illustrate the three stages of Ing. Carcano's V8 masterpiece. Here it is shown in 1955 with hand-beaten alloy 'dustbin' fairing and seat

Ultimate development of Carcano's famous flat-single—the 1957 349 cc (75 × 79 mm) Moto Guzzi engine. It produced 38 bhp at 8000 rpm

was a choice of four-, five- or even *six*-speed gear clusters available, depending on the circuit or the rider's requirements. In practice, however, it was soon discovered that the massive torque generated by the V8 rendered the six-speed cluster redundant. Incidentally, this high torque figure, at low engine rpm, made the eight-cylinder engine useful on both fast and slow going.

The chrome-moly tubular frame was of the double-cradle type, the pivot point for the round-

The V8 in 1956, with neater fairing and stacked exhaust pipes

section swinging arm being incorporated in the crankcase casting to reduce the machine's overall wheelbase. As was the practice with the majority of post-war Guzzi racing machinery, the V8 employed leading-link forks. However, in an attempt to tame the awesome power output, additional, exposed shock absorbers were fitted at the front. Besides being able to cope with the speed while in full flight,

the rider had to be in a position to halt that progress quickly. Here, Carcano's multi had the answer in the form of a massive 240 mm drum front brake, which sported four-leading-shoe operation. The rear brake was a 220 mm, single-leading shoe drum.

The fuel tank was made from hand-beaten aluminium, together with the streamlining; at first, the latter was a fully-streamlined 'dustbin', but later changed to a less-enveloping dolphin type. This

The 1957 V8, as used in the Senior TT by Dickie Dale

change of fairing came about because the dolphin was found to improve the machine's handling, particularly in adverse conditions.

The weight of 135 kg (297 lb) was truly remarkable for such a complex piece of machinery. It disproved the theory that more cylinders meant more weight!

Ing. Carcano, his two design assistants and a team of eight mechanics considered 1956 to be part of the V8's development period, and actual race successes were very limited. In fact, the machine's first victory did not come until the following year when, during the first round of the Italian Senior Championship held on 19 March 1957, over the 5.5-km (3.4-mile) Syracuse circuit in Sicily, Giuseppe Colnago won the 500 cc race at an average speed of 93.15 mph.

Then, without any special tuning or resorting to special fuels, the 1955 and 1956 350 cc World Champion, Bill Lomas, sprinted the bike along the Terracina Straight to smash the world standing-start 10-km record at an average speed of 151.5 mph, a record which still stood over three decades later! Unfortunately, an injury sustained while racing was to keep Lomas out of the action for most of that year.

Dickie Dale rode the machine in the Isle of Man TT, completing the last six-and-a-half laps on seven pots due to a burnt-out piston. He knew something

Bill Lomas astride the Guzzi V8, during a record-breaking session on Latina Straight, near Rome, March 1957

was wrong, but as the entry had been made for test purposes only, he decided to carry on until it stopped, which it did not (in an eight-lap, 302-mile race too!).

During the Belgian GP, the V8 was timed at 178 mph, by far the fastest maximum speed of any machine of this period. However, after setting the fastest lap at 118.06 mph, rider Keith Campbell was forced to retire with, of all things, a broken battery terminal.

Racing accidents sidelined the top Guzzi stars for the final Grand Prix of 1957 at Monza, and the factory decision to pull the plug on the race effort shortly afterwards prevented the V8 from ever showing its full potential. However, Guzzi did send an engine unit to England for Bill Lomas, the idea being to use it in a Formula 3 car, but this project never got off the ground. Gentleman that he is, Lomas returned the engine to Mandello where, together with a complete machine, it is on display in the factory museum.

If the V8 had been continued, the early faults which dogged it—carburation, crankshaft and lubrication—would have finally been licked. Carcano had already made preparations for racing in 1958 and had spent a lot of time making the engine respond at all throttle openings. He had also beaten the lubrication problems by fitting two additional oil pumps, while Hirth had come up with a much-improved crankshaft. There was even a 348 cc (36 × 41 mm) version, which had already been tested and found to produce 52 bhp, together with a project for a 350 four (the front block of the V8), along with a similar 250. Sadly, all these exciting ideas died with Guzzi's decision to quit racing at the end of 1957.

Thereafter, it was left to men like the leading British Guzzi privateer Arthur Wheeler who, with 250 and 350 ex-works single-cylinder engines (housed in his own Reynolds-made frames), continued to fly the flag into the 1960s. Wheeler finally retired at the end of 1962, but not before taking a

Right
Lomas again, this time proving just how compact (and light!) the Guzzi V8 engine really was

Below
Guzzi 500 V8, as ridden to fourth place in the 1957 Senior TT by Dickie Dale—on only seven cylinders!

magnificent third place in the 250 World Championship that year, which included victory in the Argentinian GP.

As for Guzzi itself, it finally came back to tarmac sport in 1969 with a series of record-breakers based on the then-new V7 V-twin roadster. Later, in the early 1970s, specially-prepared versions of the V7 Sport were campaigned by factory riders in the long endurance races of the day; perhaps the most notable of these was the prestigious Imola 200-miler in April 1972, where Guzzi finished eighth, tenth and eleventh.

However, none of these activities could match the glorious achievements which the company had garnered in its Grand Prix years.

As Bill Lomas commented in an article by journalist Charlie Rous for *Motorcycle Racing* magazine in the early 1980s: 'Japan has gained its success with money for endless labour and colossal resources. Guzzi did it with the genius of just one man—Giulio Carcano (he was referring to his time with the company during 1955-7) and his team of only eleven dedicated mechanics. I wonder what they could do today? I bet the old Guzzi team could still come up with something totally different from the rest, and they would still win.'

Lomas spoke from the heart. He, and thousands of others, *believed* that this dedicated band of engineers had been responsible for building some of the world's greatest ever racing motorcycles. Never was a truer word spoken.

Top
Arthur Wheeler raced both 250 and 350 Guzzis, which used special frames constructed by Reynolds Tubing

Above
Crankshaft flywheels from Arthur Wheeler's 350 Guzzi single

Overleaf
Arthur Wheeler, winner of the 250 cc class of the IoM Southern 100 races, July 1962. He went on to win the Argentine GP and finish third in the World Championship table that year, before announcing his retirement

Works 750 Guzzi of the type used in the 1972 Imola 200 by Vittorio Brambilla (eighth), Jack Findlay (tenth) and Guido Mandracci (eleventh)

7
Mondial

One marque of machine totally dominated the early years of the 125 cc World Championship series—FB Mondial. During 1949, 1950 and 1951 the diminutive blue and silver bikes simply ran away with the title, beating much bigger and richer teams.

The two personalities who made this happen were Count Giuseppe Boselli and Ing. Alfonso Drusiani. Giuseppe Boselli, together with his older brothers (Carlo, Luigi and Ettore), had founded the FB (Fratelli Boselli—Brothers Boselli) company in Milan during 1929 to sell, first, GD two-stroke lightweights and later four-stroke CM models. Guiseppe also rode one of the latter machines to win a gold medal in the

The all-conquering 125 dohc Mondial won a trio of world titles in 1949, 1950 and 1951. Pictured is the machine used by Gianni Leoni to win the 1949 Italian GP at Monza

1935 ISDT. Just prior to the outbreak of World War 2, the company had begun production of its own three-wheel truck. The majority of components for these vehicles were manufactured in Bologna, where FB had opened a small workshop, which Giuseppe Boselli visited frequently.

It was in Bologna, shortly after the war, that he encountered the gifted engineer Drusiani. The conversation which led to the creation of the Mondial marque took place between the two in a Bologna café during January 1948.

At that time, the two-stroke ruled supreme in the ultra-lightweight racing category, but Drusiani firmly believed that the all-conquering MV Agusta and Morini 125 'strokers' could easily be beaten by a four-stroke with double overhead camshafts.

This was an innovative argument, as in those days nobody else considered it remotely possible. How-

Carlo Ubbiali on a 125 Mondial during the 125 cc Dutch TT at Assen, 23 June 1952. He finished runner-up to MV-mounted Cecil Sandford. Note how similar it was to the 1949 version

ever, Count Boselli was attracted to the idea, so much so that he agreed to create a small racing department within FB's Bologna workshop.

Ing. Drusiani was soon installed and immediately began transferring his concept from mere dreams into reality. He was assisted by the Count, who was an able engineer in his own right and had been responsible, over the years, for several interesting features on both touring and racing machinery.

The prototype of the new design was ready by the middle of 1948, and it fully justified the confidence lavished upon its birth. The two overhead camshafts were driven by a vertical tower shaft, with straight-cut bevel gears, on the offside of the cylinder, while the 80-degree-inclined, special steel valves employed exposed 2.5 mm diameter hairpin springs. Both the cylinder and head were cast in light alloy, with an austenitic liner and steel valve seats.

For its day, the 9:7:1 compression ratio was the highest possible, being limited by the enforced use of low-grade 80-octane petrol, which was all that was available at the time. The forged, high-dome piston employed three piston rings (two compression and one oil scraper).

The 123.54 cc (53 × 56 mm) engine was slightly long-stroke, but it still managed to rev safely to 8000 rpm, at which point it pumped out almost 11 bhp. When one considers that the very best two-strokes could only manage a maximum of 10 bhp—after years of development—it can be seen that the newcomer offered real potential.

The Marelli magneto was in front of the crankcase and gear driven, as was the oil pump, which was fed oil from a tank mounted atop the fuel tank, à la Moto Guzzi. A cover on the nearside of the engine concealed the outside flywheel. The technical specification was completed by a geared primary drive, multi-plate clutch, 22 in. alloy wheel rims, plunger rear suspension and blade-type front forks with a central spring.

With a dry weight of only 88.50 kg (195 lb), the FB Mondial was a truly diminutive machine. Not only did it make the very best use of an excellent power-to-weight ratio, but it also demanded an equally small jockey.

The fledgling racer's début came in the 1948 Italian GP, which was staged at Faenza, the Monza Autodrome being still out of action due to war damage. With Franco Lama in the saddle, it displayed a clean pair of heels to the works MVs and Morinis, setting the fastest lap for its class, but then it was forced to retire with, of all things, a leaking fuel tank!

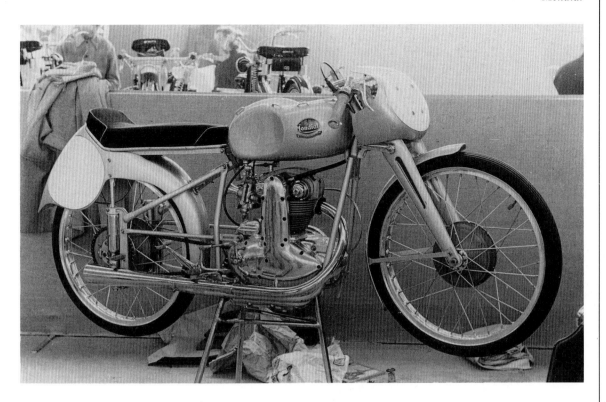

Above
Mondial single-overhead-cam 125 cc production racer, Swiss show 1953

Below
Mountside Hairpin, Scarborough, July 1954. Maurice Cann with his privately-entered, Earles-forked, double-knocker 125 Mondial

Left
Reflections in the rain. An unusual shot of Cecil Sandford with his 250 double-knocker Mondial at Aintree, 28 September 1957

Right
The 1957 250 cc World Champion and Mondial rider, Cecil Sandford

Overleaf
The fastest man in the 125 and 250 cc races at the 1957 Belgian Grand Prix, Tarquinio Provini, set new lap records in both classes. Although he won the 125 cc event, his 250, seen here, failed to last the distance. Note front and rear streamlining

One month later, still without any form of streamlining, it was taken out in the most awful weather (mist and heavy rain) on a deserted road near Cremona for Gino Cavanna (nicknamed the 'Flying Monk') to set new world records for the 125 cc class in both the flying and standing-start kilometre and mile distances. Speeds included 80.8 mph for the flying kilometre.

By the autumn, Monza was back in action and, with the Italian Grand Prix already run, an event counting towards the domestic Senior Championship was arranged. This drew all the leading Italian machines and riders of the day, but the Mondial, now in the hands of the very experienced Nello Pagani, completely blitzed the opposition to win easily. With its maximum speed raised to 90 mph, it was the star of the meeting . . . the *Bialbero* (double-cam) Mondial was on its way.

For the 1949 season, Ing. Drusiani had managed to bump the power up still further to 13 bhp at 9500 rpm. This resulted in the two-strokes being left even further behind, and Pagani had little difficulty in taking the newly-instituted 125 cc World Championship crown, coming home first in two of the three rounds, in Switzerland and Holland. The third was won by team-mate Gianni Leoni, who averaged 77.8 mph for the 113.4-kilometre (70.4-mile) race at the Grand Prix des Nations at Monza in September.

In the same year—with streamlining, but without a supercharger and still running on low-grade petrol—Cavanna improved considerably on his previous year's performances over the flying kilometre and mile, hoisting the speed to just over 100 mph. This time, the venue was outside Italy, on the newly-completed Brussels–Ostend autoroute.

Rivals Morini and MV both turned to four-strokes for 1950, and to combat this new menace, Alfonso

Drusiani improved the double-knocker Mondial still further. With 15 bhp at 11,500 rpm, the opposition was vanquished yet again.

A new signing for the Mondial team came in time for the 1950 season and took the form of Carlo Ubbiali, who had previously ridden two-stroke MVs in both races and trials. He soon showed his worth to Count Boselli by coming second in the World Championship to another new signing, Bruno Ruffo (the 1949 250 cc Champion on a Moto Guzzi), and winning the Italian Senior Championship title.

Once more, only three events counted towards the world title and, oddly enough, Ubbiali achieved his first ever Mondial victory in the Ulster GP, while Ruffo won in Holland and Leoni at Monza. Ruffo, Ubbiali and Leoni—in that order—also took the first three places for Mondial in the championship table. Meanwhile Pagani, who was still in the team, won the Spanish GP, although this was a non-championship event.

In 1950 FB Mondial had also joined the ranks of mainstream motorcycle manufacturers when it commenced the sale of a roadster to the public. The machine was a 125 cc pushrod model, which otherwise shared a family likeness with the works racing bikes.

For the 1951 season, Mondial employed Leoni, Alberti, Pagani and Ubbiali, plus its first foreign

Ex-works 250 Mondial raced so successfully by Mike Hailwood in 1959 and 1960

riders—Englishman Len Parry and Ulsterman Cromie McCandless (brother of Rex, the designer of the legendary Norton Featherbed frame). The two 'foreigners' had been recruited expressly because of the Isle of Man, this being the first time that 125 cc machines were to compete over the famous mountain course. Moreover, McCandless would have been World Champion had not the Ulster GP result been excluded from the final placing because too few riders had taken part. As it was, Ubbiali took the first of his many titles, followed by Leoni and McCandless.

For 1951 Ing. Drusiani had further boosted the power output of the little double-overhead-cam motor to a heady 16 bhp at 12,000 rpm and, once again, the combined challenge of MV and Morini was unable to counter this. However, the following year was totally different, as not only had MV greatly improved its design, but also in Les Graham and Cecil Sandford, had two of the finest pilots around. Furthermore, Morini had a youngster called Emilio Mendogni—Mondial had sat on its laurels at just the wrong moment. The result was that, for the first time, a company other than Mondial (MV

Agusta) won the 125 cc world title. Thus Ubbiali, still the best of the Mondial men, had to make do with coming second to Sandford in the World Championship, although he managed to retain his Italian title.

In 1953 not only did Ubbiali quit the team to ride for rival MV, but Drusiani had lost much of his enthusiasm. This effectively halted Mondial in its tracks. In Italy Mendogni and Morini swept the board, while abroad, as was to be the case in 1954, the mighty German NSU company simply won everything.

Meanwhile, Mondial turned its attention to sports machine racing and to the sale of over-the-counter 'customer racers'. The first model to go on sale was a 125 based on the successful works machines, except that it had a single overhead cam and a lower state of engine tune. One of the first buyers to take delivery was the then unknown Tarquinio Provini from Cadeo, in Northern Italy.

After racing an old MV two-stroke under his uncle's name (because he was not old enough to qualify!), Tarquinio finally 'came of age' and obtained the 125 Mondial. In 1953 he won every race in which he competed, a performance which gained him a place as an official works rider for 1954.

He started the year in great style, winning the

arduous eight-day, 1989-mile Giro d'Italia (Tour of Italy). The Mondial was basically one of the smaller engines bored to 66 mm, increasing the capacity to 175 cc, while the stroke remained the same at 56 mm. The result was an engine which produced in excess of 20 bhp and revved to over 9000 rpm in complete safety.

Other modifications included coil ignition, wet-sump lubrication and a more modern set of cycle parts. The last included telescopic front forks and swinging-arm rear suspension.

By the end of the season, Count Boselli considered that Provini was ready for international competition, so entries were made for the final two rounds of the 1954 125 cc World Championship series. The first took place at Monza, where the young Mondial rider split a pack of works MVs (there were no NSUs following Ruppert Hollaus' fatal crash in practice) to finish a brilliant runner-up to race winner Sala, and in front of former Mondial idol Ubbiali. During his début on foreign soil, Provini went one better and won the final round in Spain, over the twists and turns of Montjuich Park, Barcelona.

It should be noted that Provini's mount had a 'new' engine, which looked quite different from the one that had given Mondial so much success in the early years. Although it still retained the original's bore and stroke measurements, and dohc with shaft and bevel-gear drive (although experiments were

carried out with gear distribution), it produced slightly more power (17 bhp) and had a different crankcase that contained the lubricating oil—as on the 175. Also, like the larger mount, the chassis had been redesigned and sported the more modern, and more efficient, fully-damped suspension on both wheels, together with 19 in. wheels.

Finally, the latest 125 Mondial Grand Prix had a five-speed transmission and an improved aircooled clutch. Maximum speed—with comprehensive streamlining—was almost 110 mph.

However, as events were to prove during the following year, nothing short of a completely new engine would have been enough to stay with the fast-improving twin-cam MVs. Besides Provini, Mondial had also signed Ferri and Lattanzi for the 1955 title fight, but Ferri's runner-up spot in the opening round in Spain was the company's best placing.

Much of the reason for this lack of success can be placed firmly on a new 250 of which designer Drusiani and Count Boselli had great hopes.

The 250 was a *twin* and stemmed from the fact

Silverstone, 22 August 1959. Left to right: Mike Hailwood (Mondial), Tommy Robb (GMS) and Jim Adams (Mondial). The trio took first, second and third respectively in the 250 cc Championship race. The fastest lap went to Hailwood at 89.4 mph

that an overbored 175, with a capacity of 216 cc, had proved totally uncompetitive in Grand Prix events. Thus, work began in earnest on a full-size 250 during the autumn of 1955. Essentially, it employed a pair of 125 cc cylinders mounted on a common crankcase. The bore and stroke measurements were slightly long-stroke at 53 × 56 mm, giving a capacity of 248.08 cc.

Although its engine was *claimed* to produce 35 bhp at 10,000 rpm (which was almost equal to the all-conquering NSU Rennmax), the Mondial was hampered by a dry weight of 136 kg (300 lb), which was far too heavy. Another factor was that to achieve the high power output, Drusiani had been forced to virtually over-tune, the result being an extremely narrow power-band, which needed a six-speed transmission.

In the end, although two complete machines were constructed, it proved a time-wasting (and costly!) exercise, which is only remembered today because of its fully-enclosed Campagnolo single disc brake. The 250 Mondial was the first ever racing motorcycle to use such a device.

After wasting virtually two years on the ill-fated twin, Mondial made a huge effort to catch up for the 1957 season. For a start, Cecil Sandford and Sammy Miller were recruited into the Milanese team

Sixth finisher in the 1965 250 cc TT, David Williams on one of the two ex-Hailwood Mondials at Waterworks

to join Provini. The relatively small factory was rewarded by Provini and Sandford getting the season off to a flying start by winning a TT race apiece, then going on to beat the MV teamsters throughout the season. This concluded with Tarquinio becoming World Champion in the 125 cc class, while Cecil took the title in the larger category; Provini also became Italian champion in both classes.

On the technical front, Drusiani and his team of mechanics, worked long and hard to update the 125 and design a totally new 250 single. The smaller bike lost its outside flywheel and gained a seven-speed gearbox, plus many other improvements. Although the 125 retained its shaft and bevel gears, the new 250 featured camshafts which were driven by a train of gears. Actual capacity was 249.16 cc (75 × 56.4 mm), and it offered a choice of five, six or seven gears. Maximum power was 29 bhp at 10,800 rpm; with full streamlining, it could top 135 mph.

Perhaps the unluckiest moment of the entire season (at least for Sammy Miller) was when, with the 250 cc TT in his grasp, the Ulsterman fell on the last corner, almost within sight of the flag, letting Sandford through to victory. Miller finally pushed in to finish fifth, his accident having been caused by a siezed gearbox.

At the Italian GP at Monza, Mondial tested a desmodromic (positive valve operation), four-cam version of the 125 cc model, while Provini won a fiercely-contested 250 cc race after stiff opposition

In the early and mid 1960s, Mondial built and raced—with the help of the Villa brothers—various disc-valve two-strokes. This is the 1966 125 twin. There was also a 250 twin and a 125 single

from MV Agusta and Moto Guzzi. All seemed set for a period of domination by Count Boselli's bikes.

However, it was not to be. Together with Gilera and Guzzi, Mondial made the shock announcement, in October 1957, that it was withdrawing from racing. Sad news indeed. Quite simply, the vast costs of running a racing team could not be balanced by the sales of the company's bread-and-butter production machines—sales were falling, costs were rising.

In truth, sporting inactivity lasted for three years. Then, Francesco Villa, working in the Bologna experimental department, persuaded the management to let him remove the dust sheets from the 1957 mounts. The 250 cc model (two of which had been sold to the wealthy Stan Hailwood for his son Mike to ride in Britain) did not prove too competitive against the latest bikes in Italy, but the 125 was good enough for Villa to win the 1961, 1962, and 1963 Italian Senior Championships.

Meanwhile, Hailwood rode the Mondial to numerous victories on British short circuits, before being recruited into the Honda and MV teams during

the early 1960s.

In 1962 the factory introduced a machine with which to contest the newly-introduced 50 cc class. Débuted by Franco Villa at the first round of the World Championship in Spain, its engine is best described as a miniature version of the 125 cc double-knocker unit. With a bore and stroke of 40×39.5 mm, it displaced 49.9 cc. Peak power was developed at 13,500 rpm and delivered through a six-speed gearbox. The engine's exhaust note would have done justice to a single-cylinder 500 cc engine!

Tests were also carried out with a desmo version, but against the Suzuki and Kreidler two-strokes, it simply was not quick enough. This, in turn, led Mondial—strongly prompted by Villa—into investigating the two-stroke path.

The company's first effort in this direction made its first public appearance at Monza in September 1963, when a prototype for the 125 cc class appeared during practice for the Italian GP, ridden, of course, by that man Villa. Technically, it broke completely new ground for Mondial by being a 'stroker'. It must have come as a shock to many observers because the factory had earlier been instrumental in defeating the two-stroke challenge and pioneering the four-stroke engine in the first days of the 125 cc World Championship series.

At the time, the pundits openly accused Villa and Mondial of 'borrowing' ideas from MZ and Zündapp. However, to my mind, a much closer relative was the very similar Parilla, which first appeared in 1960 (see Chapter 11). It is interesting to relate that there was a German link, as much of the design work was carried out for Mondial by two-stroke expert Peter Durr.

The prototype that appeared at Monza sported a radial cylinder head and four-speed gearbox. When it was first raced in the spring of 1964, however, the head was square, with flat finning, and the gearbox sported eight speeds.

Otherwise, surprisingly little had been changed, the 123.67 cc (54 × 54 mm) horizontal disc-valve single having a watercooled cylinder barrel only. It produced a healthy 24 bhp at 11,000 rpm. With a low weight of only 80 kg (176 lb), the little Mondial proved sufficiently competitive to clean up in Italian events, if not the World Championship.

It was not without fault, however, being extremely difficult to ride. Not only did it have a narrow power-band, but also the additional nuisances of a hand-operated pump (providing supplementary lubrication) and a cut-out button for gear changing.

The 1965 version saw some of these problems solved, with watercooling of both the cylinder and head, and a wider torque band. Even though the power had been *reduced* by 1 bhp, the bike was more competitive, if for no other reason than that it was much easier to ride.

Even so, Villa (who was assisted by his brother, Walter) decided to take the two-stroke concept a stage further with a pair of brand-new twins. Although still disc-valve equipped and watercooled, their cylinders were vertical, not horizontal. Furthermore, they reverted to the use of aircooled heads.

Both machines employed eight-speed gearboxes (a development of the type used on the horizontal singles) with a dry clutch, battery/coil ignition and a mechanically-operated supplementary oil pump, which was driven by the crankshaft. This pump was particularly appreciated because it did away with the nuisance of the hand-operated pump used on the singles.

After a disagreement between Mondial and Franco Villa, the latter left (taking the 250 twin design with him!) to work and race for the Spanish Montesa concern. Meanwhile, Walter Villa returned, after a short and unsuccessful period with MV, to ride the new 125 Mondial twin, which was not race ready until early in 1966.

Bore and stroke measurements were 43 × 43 mm, the compression ratio 12:1, and maximum power 30 bhp at 14,000 rpm. There were two 27 mm Dell'Orto carburettors. The light-alloy crankcase, split horizontally, contained four main bearings.

The riders were Walter Villa and Giuseppe Mandolini. Villa was the most successful, winning the Senior Italian title in both 1966 and 1967. However, these excellent results were not gained on the new twin, but an updated version of the horizontal single. The twin had been put to one side because of unreliability.

The final Mondial racing design of the classic era appeared in the Milan show at the end of 1967, when the company displayed an aircooled, 50 cc, single-cylinder two-stroke racer with piston-port induction that produced 10 bhp at 12,000 rpm. Other details included Campagnolo disc brakes, a miniature duplex chassis, a six-speed gearbox and a branched exhaust pipe with two expansion chambers.

Unfortunately, by this time, the company was beginning to experience financial problems and the design was not developed further. A sad end to a racing effort which had been filled with so many magic moments during the immediate post-war era, which had culminated in that glorious 125/250 cc double-championship year of 1957.

8

Morbidelli

Born in 1938, Giancarlo Morbidelli grew up with a deep passion for racing motorcycles. His teens were spent during the 1950s, the 'golden era' of Italian participation in the sport.

During the 1960s the young Morbidelli built up a thriving woodworking machinery factory in his home town of Pesaro, on the Adriatic Coast, a short distance from the Benelli works. A combination of enthusiasm, finance and the desire to gain publicity for his business saw Giancarlo join the list of racing entrants in 1968, at the age of 30. He entered a modified Benelli 60 and a Motobi that Luciano Mele used to win the Italian Junior Championship.

From this relatively small beginning came the concept of developing his own machines which, in turn, was to lead to the ultimate glory of World Championship success. In late 1968 Giancarlo Morbidelli took the decision to build a completely new 50 cc racer with the help of Franco Ringhini, who had recently left the Guazzoni factory.

The riders of the newcomer were to be Eugenio Lazzarini (who had earlier raced the Morbidelli-sponsored 60 cc Benelli) and Ringhini himself. Not only did this duo finish first and second during the machine's début at an international meeting in Yugoslavia, but Lazzarini also gained the marque's first

The first autonomous Morbidelli racer was this watercooled 50 with disc-valve induction and six-speed gearbox. During 1969 it was ridden by its designer, Franco Ringhini, and also by Eugenio Lazzarini

Morbidelli works rider Gilberto Parlotti leading the 1972 125 TT, shortly before his fatal accident on the second lap of the race

World Championship points in the same year, with a sixth place in the East German GP at the Sachsenring!

Designed by Ringhini, the 1969 Morbidelli featured a single-cylinder two-stroke engine of 49.8 cc (40 × 39.8 mm) with disc-valve induction, water-cooling and a six-speed gearbox. The carburettor was a 24 mm Dell'Orto. This first pure-bred Morbidelli pumped out 10 bhp at 14,500 rpm, giving a top speed of 99 mph.

For the following season, Giancarlo decided to go one rung further up the capacity ladder and produce a 125 cc machine. As before, this was the responsibility of Franco Ringhini.

Using the 39.8 mm stroke of the 50, he increased the bore size to 44.4 mm to provide a combined capacity for both cylinders of 121.03 cc. Once again, there was the tried and tested formula of disc-valve induction, watercooling and six speeds.

The hard-chromed-bore alloy cylinders were inclined forward 23 degrees from the vertical, while other technical details include a multi-plate dry clutch, high-level expansion chambers, coil ignition, Fontana brakes and Ceriani suspension. Carburation requirements were taken care of by a pair of 27 mm SSI Dell'Ortos, and the maximum power output was in the region of 30 bhp.

At its début at Modena, in March 1970, designer/rider Franco Ringhini finished fifth, being just beaten by Britain's Chas Mortimer on a works Villa. Thus, the twin-cylinder Morbidelli clearly showed that it had true potential. This was given a tremendous boost when new signing Gilberto Parlotti rode the bike to victory in the 125 cc Czech Grand Prix at Brno, giving Italy its first win in the class since Carlo Ubbiali's 1960 victories on MVs.

For 1970 the 50 cc single received more tuning, the result being a power increase to 13.5 bhp at 14,500 rpm and 105 mph. However, with the new 125 twin getting most of the attention, Lazzarini's fifth place in the opening round of the title chase, at the Nürburgring, was its best result.

In 1971 Morbidelli fielded machines in the 50 cc class for Alberto Jeva, and in the 125 cc class for Parlotti. Jeva's ninth in the Italian GP was the only placing in the top ten in a classic that year, the result being a Morbidelli withdrawal from the 50 cc class.

Things were very different in the 125 cc class, however, Parlotti starting off in fine style with a couple of runner-up positions in Austria and West Germany. Then, a series of mechanical problems caused a host of retirements, which put him out of the title hunt. A comeback was achieved when Parlotti beat a star-studded field—which included the likes of Barry Sheene, Angel Nieto and Dave Simmonds—to win on home ground at Monza in September.

Then came 1972 . . . Gilberto Parlotti amazed the racing world by not only finishing in each of the first four rounds of the World Championship series, but also scoring two wins (at Nürburgring and Clermont-Ferrand), a second (at Salzburg) and a third (Imola).

The Isle of Man TT followed, and at that time still

This 1973 350 narrow-angle V4 Morbidelli never went beyond the prototype stage, following a similar fate to another four-cylinder model in the previous year

Members of the 1975 Morbidelli development team. Chief designer Jorg Möller is seated on the latest 125 disc-valve twin which, by then, was producing well over 40 bhp

Crankcase, crankshaft, gears and clutch from the 1976 125 cc Morbidelli twin

counted towards the Championship. The 32-year-old motorcycle dealer from Trieste (unlike his main rival Angel Nieto) decided to race in the TT for the first time in an effort to establish a lead in the closely-contested title race.

The Morbidelli star, who had also ridden for Ducati, Tomos and Benelli, arrived several days before practice and covered well over 50 laps of the mountain circuit on a 750 Ducati V-twin roadster before official training started. However, disaster was waiting in the wings. Leading a wet 125 cc TT by 18 seconds from Mortimer (Yamaha) on lap 2, Parlotti was killed instantly when he crashed at the Verandah.

The accident was to have profound consequences, both within the Morbidelli camp and in the racing world as a whole. Not only did it halt the team's bid for the 1972 125 cc title, but it also brought about an exodus of stars, led by Agostini, from the TT. This, in turn, brought an end to the event counting towards the mainstream World Championships.

Parlotti had also been secretly testing a new four-cylinder 350 cc Morbidelli. Like the smaller bikes, the four was a watercooled, disc-valve two-stroke, but otherwise the design was totally different. The engine featured transverse, inclined cylinders that were parallel to the ground. There were two disc valves (one at each end of the crankcase) and four

carburettors. The majority of the engine castings were in electron alloy. These, combined with a very lightweight frame, meant that it was the lightest machine in its class.

Originally to have been raced by Parlotti in September 1972, the design was eventually scrapped and superseded by a totally new machine. About the only thing the replacement shared with the original was its engine size.

The 1973 350 four-cylinder Morbidelli is best described as two separate engines in 'piggy-back' formation—in other words, one superimposed on the other. All four cylinders faced forward, and each had its own rotating disc. The watercooled assembly had two separate crankshafts, plus a countershaft to drive the coolant pump. In its original prototype form, it offered a class-topping 85–90 bhp at 14,000 rpm, which was some 25 per cent greater than anything in existence at the time. However, it was soon discovered that the engine had one serious fault—excessive vibration. Unfortunately, after much experimentation and testing, it was found that the only way of effectively removing this was to reduce the power output by a large amount. Therefore, after considerable cost, the whole project was axed.

Other technical details of this most interesting design included a six-speed gearbox, four 30 mm Japanese Mikuni carburettors, special Motoplat electronic ignition, a duplex frame and a four-

Connecting rod and piston from the 1976 125 twin

leading-shoe front brake. The dry weight was 130 kg (286 lb).

However, if the four-cylinder 350 did not progress, the 125 cc model most certainly did, but it took some time for Morbidelli to find a suitable man to replace Parlotti.

During the latter part of 1972, several riders were tested, including Otello Buscherini, Chas Mortimer and, most notably, Angel Nieto. The last had won both the 50 and 125 cc world titles that year on Derbi machinery, but in November the Spanish company announced that it was making a complete withdrawal from World Championship events.

After testing the 125 twin at Modena, in early December, Nieto signed a contract to race in both 125 and 350 cc classes for the Pesaro team. This was despite the fact that he had stated that he did not like the handling or the streamlining of the smaller bike, and had been unable to test the bigger machine.

Morbidelli agreed to modify the frame and to build new fairings. The streamlining was tested in the brand-new wind-tunnel which had just been installed at the factory of car-styling specialists Pininfarina.

Much was expected of the new pairing, but Nieto retired more times than he finished on the 125, and he never rode the 350. All hopes of glory soon evaporated. The tiny Spanish superstar quit the team as soon as his contract expired at the end of the season and joined Bultaco.

Two very important events for Morbidelli occurred in 1974—the signature of Paolo Pileri as rider, and the decision to employ a new designer. Both moves were to bear fruit in the following year.

The new engineer was the widely-travelled and respected Jorg Möller who, together with Franco Dionsi, Luigi Cecchini and Giancarlo Bonaventura, evolved a team of 'back-room boys' to challenge the best. Möller joined Morbidelli on 28 February 1974 from the Dutch Van Veen team.

Morbidelli works rider Paolo Pileri in the process of winning the 1976 125 cc Italian Grand Prix at Mugello

By the time the latest 125 twin was ready for action, most of the season had passed by. However, proof of its potential came when Pileri scored an impressive second place to the 1974 125 cc World Champion, Kent Anderson, at the Czech GP. The real target, however was 1975, and Möller openly said that he was tipping Pileri as the next champion.

To provide additional support, Morbidelli also signed Pier-Paolo Bianchi, who had finished third in the 1974 125 cc Italian GP at Imola on a Minarelli. Bianchi soon proved his worth when he won the final 125 race to be staged in Italy in October. At that time, the best Morbidelli 125 watercooled twin was producing 39 bhp, but Möller predicted that this would be over 40 bhp before the start of the new season.

So it proved, the 124.1 cc (43.9 × 41 mm) disc-valve twin pumping out 42 bhp at 14,200 rpm. Möller's recipe for success was to employ the very best materials from all over Europe. For example, the single-ring forged pistons came from Mahle in Germany, while the Hoekle hardened-steel crankshaft came from the same country. The light-alloy barrels had Nikasil bores for long life under racing conditions. There were four nylon-caged main bearings, and needle rollers were used for both the big- and small-ends. The Mahle pistons featured a single chrome 1 mm thick ring and gave a compression ratio of 15:1. Lubrication was by petroil mixture at a ratio of 20:1. Carburation was taken care of by a

Above
The Bimota-framed Morbidelli 250 disc-valve twin

Overleaf
World Champion Mario Lega during the 250 cc Czech GP at Brno, August 1977: he finished third

pair of 28 mm choke Mikuni instruments.

In the transmission department, spur primary gears fed the power to the six-speed, all-indirect gearbox via a dry, multi-plate clutch. This featured eight sintered-bronze friction plates and seven steel driven plates.

The ignition system comprised a Krober battery-powered electronic capacitor discharge unit that fired Champion N82G spark plugs at 1 mm BTDC.

Braking was taken care of by triple 216 mm (8½ in.) diameter Brembo discs mounted on Campagnolo magnesium-alloy five-spoke wheels. The tyres were Michelin PZ8 M38 2.75 × 18. The suspension was Marzocchi—telescopic front fork with magnesium sliders, and pivoted rear fork controlled by gas dampers that offered five-position spring preload adjustment at the rear.

A Krober electronic tacho, calibrated 6–16,000 rpm, enabled the rider to keep the peaky engine on the boil, its power-band being between 10,000 and 14,200 rpm. The VDO 40–100°C temperature gauge needed to read between 60 and 70°C for effective working temperature.

With a dry weight of 75 kg (165 lb), the blue and white flyer was capable of around 145 mph on optimum gearing at ultra-fast circuits such as Spa Francorchamps, the venue for the Belgian GP.

On the track, Möller's handiwork proved not only extremely rapid, but just as importantly *reliable*. Thus, in the first eight rounds of the 1975 125 cc World Championship, Paolo Pileri finished every time—and in seven, he was the winner! With the title already won, Pileri (and team-mate Bianchi) did not even bother to compete in the other events.

This level of success brought a huge demand for replica machines from private owners. Morbidelli responded by entering into a joint agreement with Benelli Armi (the gun manufacturing company still under the control of the Benelli family).

A new factory was built in Pesaro expressly for constructing batches of the 125 watercooled disc-valve twin to sell world-wide to (wealthy!) customers. The first of these to reach Britain was purchased by Len Carr, owner of the Widerange Bearing Company in Leicestershire.

The 'customer racer' was virtually a replica of the Pileri and Bianchi works bikes, but the engines did not produce quite so much power (36.5 bhp)—Morbidelli did not want to make public all of its secrets!

Unfortunately, many riders who bought early models experienced serious crankshaft problems. These were caused by the lack of clearance between the crankpin, big-end bearing and con-rod. The result was overheating and seizure. The manufacturers of the crankshaft, Hoekle of Stuttgart, had cured this problem by mid 1976 and, thereafter, the cranks gave long and reliable service.

On the world stage, it was Bianchi's turn for title honours in 1976. He won seven races of the nine-round series, while Anton Mang of West Germany won on a 'private' bike on his home ground at the Nürburgring.

By 1977 well over half the grid of any 125 cc GP were Morbidelli-mounted, and quite often races were virtually a benefit for the tiny Pesaro marque. Only the lone special Bultaco of Angel Nieto offered any sort of a challenge.

At the end of the year, Bianchi was champion for the second year running. Moreover, Morbidelli also took the 250 cc title, thanks to the consistent Mario Lega who, although he won only a single round (Yugoslavia), was always in the points.

The 250 had first appeared mid-way through 1976 when, ridden by Pileri, it had finished runner-up to the World Champion Walter Villa's Harley-Davidson (see Chapter 1) in Belgium.

Various frames were tried, including one constructed by the Bimota concern, the definitive version employing single-shock rear suspension. The 249.7 cc (56 × 50.7 mm) twin-cylinder engine followed the familiar Morbidelli formula of disc-valve induction, watercooling and six-speed transmission. Power output was quoted as being 64 bhp at 11,500 rpm, with maximum speed 'over 160 mph'. There was also a 350 version (347.43 cc— 64 × 54 mm).

The 500 square-four Morbidelli two-stroke, as raced in 1979 by Graziano Rossi. This, together with a later V4 design, failed to achieve the success of the smaller 125 and 250 twin-cylinder models

Into 1978 and the works machines were renamed MBA (Morbidelli-Benelli Armi). In this guise, they helped Eugenio Lazzarini become the new 125 cc World Champion—but only after stiff opposition from the new Minarelli teamsters of Nieto and Bianchi.

Lega and Pileri rode the 250 and 350 twins (still entered under the Morbidelli label). However, with the exception of Pileri's brilliant victory on the 250 in Belgium, they had a poor year.

Morbidelli (read MBA) continued to garner considerable success with its long-running 125 twin well into the 1980s. In fact, they fared well until the FIM changed the rules and introduced the single-cylinder formula in 1988.

A development of the 250 twin also continued into the new decade. This was campaigned under the MBA banner, too.

Therefore, the last true Morbidelli to contest the World Championship series was a 500. In fact, there were *two* separate designs, both of which were powered by four-cylinder two-stroke engines with disc-valve induction, watercooling and six speeds.

The first of the 500s was a 'square' four, in which the cylinders were canted forward at 35 degrees. This meant that the gearbox and clutch could be moved forward *underneath* the engine. There were two crankshafts, not four as on the Suzuki RG500, and power was taken from the offside, not the centre.

Bore and stroke followed the then current square 54 × 54 mm dimensions, not the short-stroke arrangement as used on the 250. This was because the twin had always suffered from an ultra-narrow power-band; square dimensions were adopted in an attempt to provide more torque.

Many of the engine castings were of magnesium, being made by wheel and brake specialists Campagnolo. However, although the design displayed many interesting features, it did not leave the prototype stage. Instead, in 1980, it was superseded by an entirely new concept.

The later 500 was a narrow-angle (45-degree) V4 of 494.16 cc (55 × 52 mm), which was reputed to produce a staggering 130 bhp at 11,500 rpm. Other technical details included a compression ratio of 13:1, four 34 mm Mikuni carburettors, electronic ignition, an aluminium monocoque chassis, 16 in. five-spoke wheels, twin 260 mm discs at the front and a single 210 mm unit at the rear. The machine had a dry weight of 135 kg (298 lb) and a claimed maximum speed of 181 mph.

Great things were expected from the V4 and its rider Graziano Rossi, but a series of mechanical failures and crashes conspired to frustrate every effort to turn it into a competitive Grand Prix machine.

Eventually, Giancarlo Morbidelli called a halt to the project. It is uncertain whether the reason was the lack of success achieved or the high development costs. Whatever the reason, it effectively signalled the end of an effort which had carved the Morbidelli name on five World Championship titles in a few short years during the 1970s.

9
Morini

Many enthusiasts would argue that the dohc 250 Morini, which reached a peak in 1963 when the might of Honda only just managed to vanquish the lone Italian single with Tarquinio Provini in the saddle, was the most outstanding design of its type ever conceived. Whether one subscribes to this particular theory or not, it is an indisputable fact that the bike was the *fastest* single-cylinder four-stroke of its capacity ever made.

To trace the machine's history, we have to go back to the period just before the outbreak of World War 1 in 1914. It was then that Alfonso Morini, after serving an apprenticeship with a local smithy, set up a tiny motorcycle repair workshop near his home in the central Italian town of Bologna.

Morini's workshop had already managed to create something of a reputation for good engineering work by the time that he was called up for the army during

Morini's first four-stroke racer. The 1950 123.1 cc chain-driven sohc engine produced 12 bhp and could push the bike to speeds approaching 90 mph

1916. This, in turn, led directly to his gaining a posting to the car and motorcycle repair section at Padua.

The period in military service provided Alfonso Morini with an excellent chance to widen his knowledge and expertise. By the end of hostilities, he was able to return to his Bologna workshop with sufficient experience to undertake a more ambitious business venture.

Not satisfied with purely repairing machines, Morini realized that the time was ripe to enter the manufacturing side of the business. To this end, he enlisted a partner in the shape of Mario Mezzetti, someone with very much the same enthusiasm and engineering skills as himself.

The pair decided to pool their resources, production of the first MM (Morini-Mezzetti) model beginning in 1924. This initial design was a two-stroke with a capacity of 125 cc. It was equipped with a two-speed, hand-operated gearbox, girder front forks and an unsprung chassis. Soon, the pair decided to gain much needed publicity by entering Morini for as many of the numerous races that were taking place throughout Italy as possible.

A fair level of success came, too, most notably on the ultra-tough Lario circuit. This attracted other riders, notably the well-known pairing of Landi and Tigli, who soon joined forces with Morini. With the typical barnstorming spirit of the 'Roaring Twenties', they gained victories wherever they went.

Without doubt, however, the victory that was to remain the proudest moment of Alfonso Morini's own particular career was when he won his class in the 1927 Italian Grand Prix at the Monza Autodrome. After this, he tended to let others do the riding, while he spent more time with Mezzetti on the technical and management side.

During the early 1930s they, like virtually every other company in the industrial world, had to cope with the Great Depression. Even so, somehow they found the finances to produce their first four-stroke

By 1952 the single-knocker Morini was offering an additional 4 bhp and 100 mph

racer. Of 175 cc capacity, it featured a single overhead camshaft, which was driven by an enclosed chain on the offside of the engine. This chain drive not only continued while the MM partnership lasted, but also right up to the 1950s as a feature of Morini racing engine design. Another interesting aspect of the machine was the use of a British Albion gearbox.

From its very first appearance, the 175 MM was a success. Among its many wins, Lama's victory in the 1933 Italian Grand Prix was, perhaps, the most notable. It was also used in a number of record attempts with outstanding success. In the same year as Lama's Monza victory, Bonazzi secured the flying kilometre world record at a shade over 100 mph—without any form of streamlining!

A 250 cc version was also built, and even a 350 cc model. Both were as successful as the original. In 1938, for example, Mangione became Italian Senior Champion in the 350 cc category aboard one of the single-knocker MMs. However, this came a year after Morini and Mezzetti had split up.

Always something of an individualist, Morini desired to establish a factory of his own. Unfortunately, the immediate pre-war period was a difficult time for the Italian industry. Although he was ready to proceed with his plan to manufacture motorcycles, and had a new racing design on the board, for commercial reasons, he was forced to devote the factory to the manufacture of three-wheeled trucks and, as soon as war was declared, to aero engine components.

When the war was finally over, Alfonso Morini could at last turn over his partly-wrecked works exclusively to motorcycle production. In fact, he was one of the very first Italian manufacturers to put a new model on the market, a robustly-constructed, 123.1 cc (52 × 58 mm), single-cylinder two-stroke with piston-port induction and a three-speed, in-unit gearbox, wet clutch and magneto ignition. It must be said that the machine owed much to the very similar German DKW design. The specification also included girder front forks, plunger rear suspension and 19 in. wheels. Launched in 1946, it was soon followed by a pukka racing version in the following year.

One of the first riders to make a name for himself on the tiny machine was a novice by the name of Umberto Masetti, later to become a double world champion with the famous Gilera factory. Another rider to enjoy early successes on Morini's 'stroker' was a young engineer by the name of Dante Lambertini. He was to become head of the Bologna factory's racing department, and the man largely responsible for the success of the legendary double-overhead-cam 250 single.

Works rider Zinzani leads a gaggle of Mondials in the 1952 Italian Grand Prix at Monza. The race was won by another Morini rider, Emilio Mendogni

Morini was also one of the first Italian marques to race outside its homeland's frontiers after the war. Moreover, it was usually right up at the front of the pack. For example, Masetti almost had the 125 cc class of the 1948 Dutch TT sewn up, only to have a spark plug fail on the final circuit.

At home, the Morini's main challenger was the new MV Agusta—also a two-stroke at this stage. However, the Bologna team triumphed, with Masetti becoming the very first Italian Senior Champion for the 125 cc category. At the end of the season, the new double-knocker FB Morini made its début, and immediately it became clear that the two-stroke's days were numbered.

After MV and Morini were soundly beaten during the fight for the first 125 cc World Championship title in the following year (1949), both quickly switched to four-strokes.

The new Morini shared the same bore and stroke measurements as its two-stroke brother. The 1950 version offered 12 bhp from its chain-driven, single-overhead-camshaft motor. Other technical features included hairpin valve springs, dry-sump lubrication, an outside flywheel, a dry clutch and all-alloy construction of the engine unit.

Unfortunately, the new design suffered several teething troubles during its first few months of life, and it was not until 1951 that the Morini team, which by then consisted of Zinzani, Zanzi and Mendogni, began to put together any sort of result. Even so, the Mondial still remained top dog, winning its third successive world title that year.

During the winter of 1951–2, the engine was improved considerably, and power output raised to 16 bhp at 9500 rpm. On the road, this meant a genuine 100 mph. Things were looking up, and Morini's top rider, Emilio Mendogni, created something of a sensation by defeating the combined might of the Morini and MV teams to win the final two rounds of the 1952 125 cc World Championship series, in Italy and Spain.

Because of these results, many expected Morini to be a serious championship contender in the following year. However, due to a massive effort by the Germans, in the shape of NSU, the best Morini could do all year was a runner-up spot at Monza with Mendogni in the saddle.

For 1954 Morini produced an enlarged 125, on which Mendogni won the 175 cc class of the Italian Senior Championship. The Bologna marque exploited this success by switching its efforts from Grand Prix to production machine events.

The result was the excellent 175 Settebello model. This sportster was not, as might have been expected, a camshaft model, but instead a humble pushrod device and closely related to the company's standard production machines. However, it not only won races, but also sold in thousands. Thus, Morini benefited from much valuable publicity, and made a healthy profit, too!

By supporting sports machine racing, Alfonso Morini soon realized that he was on to a winner in more ways than one. Therefore, although the Settebello had done extremely well, during late 1954 thought was given to the design of a more specialized machine. The result was the Rebello which, although still of the same 175 cc category (very popular with Italian enthusiasts at the time), was otherwise a completely different motorcycle.

Unlike the Settebello, the newcomer featured a chain-driven, single-overhead-camshaft engine of particularly advanced design. Another feature was a five-speed gearbox, which was extremely rare in those days, particularly for a sports machine. There was a large 27 mm, racing-style Dell'Orto carburettor, a camshaft-driven tacho and a gear-driven oil pump. Like other Morini four-strokes of the era, it employed dry-sump lubrication.

The 1959 250 Morini single featured gear-driven overhead camshafts and produced 32 bhp at 10,500 rpm. Here mechanics fettle two examples in the factory's race department

Side views of the fabulous Morini twin-cam, single-cylinder power unit. Notable features included a unit-construction, six-speed gearbox and dry multi-plate clutch

The 172.4 cc (60 × 61 mm) engine produced 22 bhp and revved to over 9000 rpm. There was a single-cradle, open, tubular frame with Marzocchi suspension at both front and rear. Other details of interest were 19 in. wheels with Borrani alloy rims, a neatly-crafted 14-litre (3¼-gallon) fuel tank, and just enough lighting equipment to make it legal. Morini claimed a maximum speed of 105 mph.

A Rebello won the 1955 Milano-Taranto and Giro

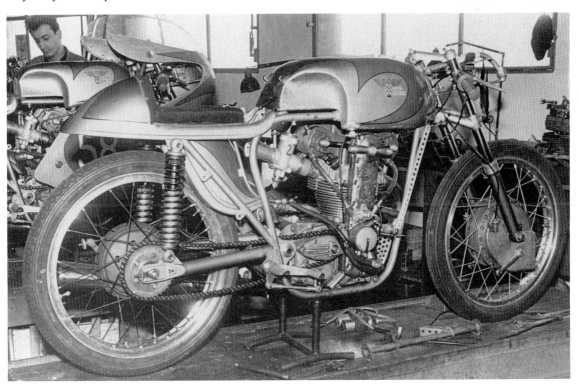

Left
Third finisher in the 1960 IoM 250 cc TT, Morini-mounted Tarquinio Provini at the approach to Governor's Bridge dip

Right
Provini's 1962 works Morini single. Note the recess in the top of the tank for his chin!

d'Italia long-distance races, and also the latter event in 1956. Morini's top rider in these and other events was Walter Tassinari.

The Rebello proved itself such a fine all-round motorcycle that a larger version with dohc was constructed for use in Grand Prix-type events. Its first race was the 1957 Italian GP. Against a hoard of works bikes from Mondial, MV Agusta and Moto Guzzi, rider Emilio Mendogni lay third for some considerable time, before being forced out through a minor technical problem.

After this impressive début, Alfonso Morini immediately authorized an extension of the development programme which had brought this prototype into existence.

The prototype engine used by Mendogni featured dohc driven by chain (as on the sohc Rebello). However, tests soon proved that a system with spur pinion drive was superior in several respects.

The actual capacity was the same on both engines: 246.667 cc (69 × 66 mm), with maximum power of 30 bhp at 10,000 rpm (120 bhp/litre) on a compression ratio of 9:5:1. The special steel connecting rod was heavily webbed at both the top and bottom, and the big-end consisted of hardened steel rollers with a light-alloy cage. Valves were of a large diameter and employed hairpin springs. There was a 30 mm SSI Dell'Orto with a remotely-mounted float chamber. Lubrication was of the traditional Morini dry-sump variety, and a double-gear pump circulated the oil.

The crankshaft had inside circular flywheels and rotated on a trio of main bearings, one of the timing side, and two for the primary drive side. Both the primary drive gears and the multi-plate clutch were contained in an oil bath.

Two ignition systems were employed—one version of the machine was fitted with a magneto; the other had a dual contact-breaker (on the offside), a battery and twin ignition coils. After extensive testing, the latter system proved superior. Both systems employed two sparking plugs.

Like that of the Rebello, the gearbox was a five-speeder and was built in-unit with the engine. The frame and cycle parts also showed strong Rebello influence. However, the front brake had been updated, a more powerful double-sided Amadoro unit having been fitted in place of the original conical, single-sided type. Dry weight was 113 kg (249 lb).

Intense development took place and, exactly 12 months to the day, Morini burst back on to the international stage with a sensational victory in the 250 cc class of the Italian Grand Prix.

The latest engine, producing 32 bhp and with gear-driven dohc, featured many modifications compared to the original prototype units. Not the least of these was the use of a six-speed gearbox.

Two of these machines were entered at Monza, with Mendogni and Zubani as riders. Mendogni led all the way and won comfortably, while Zubani annexed runner-up spot after a wheel-to-wheel dice throughout the race with MV team leader Ubbiali. During this hectic tussle, Zubani also had the satisfaction of making fastest lap at 106.30 mph.

Once again, it seemed as if Morini would do well in the following year, especially when it signed the British rider Derek Minter who, teamed with Mendogni and Zubani, promised much for the 1959 season. However, although the factory pursued an active role in entering its riders in both international

and national meetings throughout the year, successes were few—largely because of the new twin-cylinder challenge from MV and MZ, whose machines were producing considerably more power.

Surprisingly, Provini quit the MV team at the end of 1959 to become Morini's sole rider. Although he finished a notable third in the Isle of Man, his activities were confined mainly to the Italian scene. The main reason for this was the fact that a considerable test programme was taking place.

To provide the reader with a vivid insight into how such things were often conducted in those far-off (and much more relaxed!) days, here is how one journalist reported the action at the time: 'The Morini factory—situated very close to Ducati in Bologna—are working flat out to get their machines ready for the early Italian events. A few days ago one of our "spies" spotted their race van on the approach road to the *Autostrada* near Bologna. It was parked by the roadside and Provini was there with no fewer than four works machines, blasting up and down the road! Rather like trying a Manx Norton on the M1!'

This period of intense work was to prove its worth over the following years, when the 250 Morini emerged as one of the truly great racing motorcycles of all time. This was not so much because of its engine power, but because it was a *complete* package—reliability, speed, 'leech-like' handling, 'brick-wall' braking, wonderfully efficient streamlining, and exceptionally low weight.

With Provini's masterful riding talent, the combination was slowly welding into a dynamic

Left
Provini in winning form on the Morini at Modena, March 1963

Right
1963 Ulster Grand Prix, in which Provini finished second to race winner Jim Redman (Honda). These two contested the Championship throughout the season, until the final round in Japan, where the result finally went to Honda's man

Overleaf
Morini signed the up-and-coming Giacomo Agostini at the start of 1963. His main task was to fly the flag in Italy, which he did in fine style by winning the important international Shell Gold Cup at Imola. The following year he won the Senior Italian Championship for Morini, defeating his former team-mate Provini in the process

partnership—in 1961 and 1962 it won the Senior Italian Championship and enjoyed several notable results on foreign soil—so much so that Alfonso Morini decided to allow a bid to be made on the 250 cc World Championship in 1963. (This from a man who was 'not interested' in racing outside Italy!)

Even the boss of the tiny Bologna factory could never have imagined in his wildest dreams just how close the finish would be in the ten-round, 1963 250 cc World Championship.

After a full season of racing, a certain amount of bad luck (cancellation of the French GP, mechanical trouble in Holland, and the inability to obtain a visa for East Germany) and the decision to give the Isle of Man a miss, Tarquinio Provini still finished runner-up to the 250 cc World Champion Jim Redman and his mighty Honda four. Moreover, he lost the title by a mere *two* points! The vital difference on the Champion's side was the fact that he competed in the TT (which he won) and also the East German GP.

Imola again, but four years on in April 1967. Walter Villa is shown proving that the Morini single was still a force to be reckoned with by leading none other than Mike Hailwood on a six-cylinder Honda

However, Provini and Morini had the enormous satisfaction of soundly beating Redman at Monza, over the tortuous Spanish GP circuit at Montjuich Park, on the ultra-fast Hockenheim track used for the West German GP, and over the rough Buenos Aires Autodrome, thus proving the great adaptability of the design. In addition, Provini took the Italian Championship once again.

Behind the scenes, however, something of a disagreement had developed between Provini and Morini's chief engineer, Ing. Lambertini. The result was that Tarquinio quit to join Benelli at the end of the season.

After that, it was the turn of the young Giacomo Agostini to win the national title for Morini. However, he also left, this time being snapped up by Count Agusta.

Then, after a couple of years of only occasional participation in racing, with riders such as Spaggiari and Grassetti, Morini returned to championship honours in 1967 with the up-and-coming Angelo Bergamonti in the saddle.

This final success was a fitting epitaph, as the man who had been instrumental in founding not one, but two, great Italian marques died shortly after in 1969.

The definitive development of the fleet double-knocker single, which Bergamonti rode to success in 1967, had gained some 6 bhp and 500 rpm since the original prototypes of ten years before. During this time, the bore and stroke had been changed to 72×61 mm, and the capacity set at 248.36 cc.

Lambertini had been assisted by fellow engineer Biavati, who had come from the Mondial racing department and who specialized in cylinder-head work. Whilst at Morini, Biavati had experimented with desmodromic valve operation and both three- and four-valve cylinder heads. However, as if to prove that simplicity is often best, the engines which gained the championships with Provini, Agostini and finally Bergamonti had been of the conventional two-valve type.

What was of real significance was the great attention to detail and continuous testing, both on the bench and on the track. It was this, above all else, which had not only provided the extra horses, but given the design its superb reliability.

10

MV Agusta

Since the road racing World Championships were created in 1949, MV Agusta has won more titles than any other marque. Therefore, any record of Italy's post-war track achievements must also be one of the Gallarate factory itself.

MV's first classic victory, counting towards World Championship points, came at the inaugural round of the 1952 series, when Englishman Cecil Sandford won the 125 cc IoM TT. The same rider became the company's first World Champion when he took the 125 cc title that year. This was the beginning of an unparalleled run of success which spanned over a quarter of a century and saw MV win over 3000 international races, 38 individual World Championship titles and 37 manufacturers' World Championships.

The list of riders who straddled their machines reads like a *Who's Who* of motorcycle sport. It includes Cecil Sandford, Les Graham, Bill Lomas, Carlo Ubbiali, John Surtees, Luigi Taveri, Gary Hocking, Mike Hailwood, Giacomo Agostini and Phil Read.

But how did the MV story begin? To answer this, we have to go back to the year 1923, when Giovanni Agusta founded an aircraft factory at Verghera, a small village on the bleak Gallarate plain, to the

A pair of the first works MV 125 two-strokes at the 1948 Italian GP, which was staged at Faenza (Monza was still closed due to war damage). One of the bikes, ridden by Bertoni, won its class, giving the marque its first victory

Although the Gallarate factory soon came up with its own dohc 125, it continued to develop its two-strokes. This is the definitive type built in 1952. Note lengthened crankcase, needed to accommodate the magneto, which is just visible ahead of the crankshaft-mounted rotor

North of Milan. Agusta died in 1927, leaving his wife, Giuseppina, to take over the reigns of power. In this, she succeeded, ably supported by the eldest of their four sons, Domenico.

Throughout the 1930s the Agusta empire grew and prospered. Then came the war which, when it ended in 1945, left the Gallarate factory—like several other major Italian engineering concerns—without any form of work for its considerable number of employees.

Even before the end of the conflict, Domenico Agusta realized that this was going to happen and had instigated the design and construction of a prototype lightweight motorcycle, powered by a 98 cc two-stroke engine. It was to have been named the Vespa (wasp), but Piaggio had already registered this name for their freshly-created scooter. Thus, Count Agusta decided to change the name of his company from Construzioni Aeronautiche Giovanni Agusta to *Meccanica Verghera*—hence the now legendary MV initials.

A sports version of the tiny 98 cc 'stroker' made its début in 1946, and soon these were being tuned and entered by competitors in the newly-introduced 125 cc racing class, which had just been introduced in Italy.

Never a man to pass up the means of gaining publicity for his products, Count Agusta decided to build a pukka racing version with a capacity of

123.5 cc (53×56 mm). The first of these models appeared in time for the 1948 season, and later that year an example won its class at the Faenza circuit (Monza was still closed due to war damage), to give MV its first major victory.

Spurred on by this success, Count Agusta authorized an all-out crack at the 125 cc World Championship title in the following year. However, the MV two-stroke, now with several design changes to both the chassis and engine, including an increase in the power output from 9 to 10.5 bhp, could not match the new twin-camshaft FB Mondial four-stroke.

A significant development in the MV Agusta racing story came during the winter of 1949–50, when first Arturo Magni and then Ing. Piero Remor left Gilera to join the Gallarate team. This enabled MV to construct not only a brand-new 500 four-cylinder model, but ultimately their own 125 double-knocker single. Both designs were to play an important role in MV's gradual evolution into a successful racing marque.

Perhaps as was to be expected, the first four-cylinder MV, which appeared in early 1950, bore a close resemblance to the Gilera. However, Ing. Remor and his development team incorporated

The first 500 MV four appeared in 1950. Rapid development meant varying designs, including this four-carb model with Earles forks and 1951-type rear end, which was raced by team leader Les Graham at Mettet, 27 April 1952

several new features (most of which did not prove a success!). These included shaft final drive, torsion-bar suspension—both fore and aft—and gearchange levers on *both* sides of the machine. The last, rather debatable, feature called for the rider to use his heels, pushing down on the nearside for upward changes and down on the offside to change down. It was all rather unnecessary, making the rider's lot that much more difficult. Needless to say, this was soon abandoned in favour of a conventional gearchange selector on the right. The gearbox was a four-speed device built in unit with the engine and featuring a multi-plate clutch.

Bore and stroke dimensions were 'square' at 54 × 54 mm, giving a capacity of 494.4 cc. Running on a compression ratio of 9:5:1, the dohc four breathed through a pair of 28 mm Dell'Orto carburettors (two per pair of cylinders, sharing a single remote float chamber) and produced 50 bhp at 9000 rpm. With a weight of 118 kg (260 lb), the 1950 Gallarate 'fire engine' was capable of almost

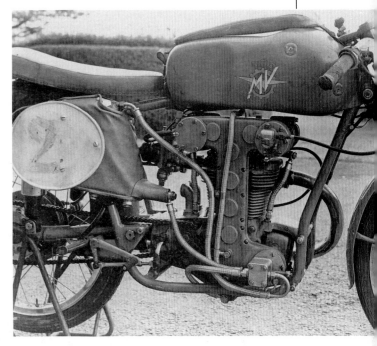

The 1953 version of the 125 twin-cam MV Agusta—it was outclassed by the all-dominant German NSUs

120 mph, making it no faster than the twin-cylinder AJS Porcupine or single-cylinder Norton.

The machine was also handicapped by its mediocre handling and roadholding qualities, but despite this, the ex-Gilera rider Arciso Artesiani managed to finish a highly-respectable third in the final round of the 1950 500 cc World Championship series at Monza, only race winner Duke (Norton) and runner-up Masetti (Gilera) leading the MV home, among a gaggle of exotic works machinery. In the main, this result was due to a high retirement rate and some determined riding on the part of Artesiani.

With the arrival of the 1949 500 cc World Champion, Les Graham, in the following winter, together with extensive development, the big MV was a much different machine when it appeared at the beginning of the 1951 season. Gone were the torsion-bar-controlled blade front forks, to be replaced by more modern teles. The weird 'double-sided', heel-operated gearchange had also been consigned to the scrap bin; finally, conventional hydraulic twin-shock suspension units replaced the original torsion-bar rear end. However, the parallelogram rear fork (double swinging arm) was retained, a feature which, Arturo Magni revealed recently, was needed because of the shaft final drive.

The Gallarate factory had three riders out on 500s that year—Graham, Bandirola and Artesiani—plus

Above
Cecil Sandford after winning the 125 cc TT in June 1952. He went on to become MV's first world champion later that year

Left
Les Graham in vivid action on the MV four at Boreham, July 1952

Works 203 cc dohc MV, as seen at the 1955 TT. Note the giant air scoop to provide adequate cooling with full streamlining fitted

The 1956 MV team. Left to right : John Surtees, Umberto Masetti, Carlo Ubbiali, Count Domenico Agusta, Angelo Copeta, Remo Venturi, Luigi Taveri and Tito Forconi

Graham and Bertoni on 125 singles. In practice, over half the classics were given a miss whilst a frantic development programme was undertaken. Artesiani again gave MV their best result, another third, this time in the Spanish GP. However, even this was something of a hollow result, as the leading riders had all been eliminated in a massive seven-bike pile-up early in the race. More worthwhile had been Graham's convincing third in the 125 cc Dutch TT at Assen, where the opposition was particularly strong.

By the end of the year, it was patently obvious that both the 500 four and 125 single were not fast enough to give the Gallarate team a chance of victory, so the race-shop engineers redoubled their efforts over the closed season.

Most notably, the engine of the four was redesigned, being given the 53×56.4 mm bore and stroke measurements of the 125 single to produce a new capacity of 497.5 cc. With larger valves, hotter cam profiles and an increase in compression ratio to 10:1, allied to four carburettors instead of two, power output rose to 56 bhp at 10,500 rpm. Moreover, the gearbox was uprated to five speeds and the drive shaft replaced by a chain. A new duplex frame, together with single rear fork, completed the picture. The result, after eradicating a few early gremlins, was the basis of a highly-competitive racing motorcycle. That year both telescopic and the new Earles-type front fork were used. Similar improvements had also been made to the 125 single.

MV camp at the 1956 TT. The machines are a mixture of 125 and 250 singles

Overleaf
John Surtees heading for victory, on the smaller 350 four, at the Belgian Grand Prix in 1956. This was the machine's first classic victory

Graham and Bandirola were retained, and several new riders signed, including the Englishman Cecil Sandford. It was Sandford who not only gave the marque its first World Championship victory in the 125 cc IoM TT, but also its first title after subsequent victories in Holland and Ulster.

Meanwhile, team leader Graham narrowly missed winning the Senior TT when, after leading, he was slowed by an oil leak towards the end of the race. Similar bad luck saw him forced to retire with tyre trouble when leading in Ulster. However, by the end of the year, Graham had proved that the big MV was a potential champion, with record-breaking victories at Monza and Barcelona. He ended the season a mere three points behind the new 500 cc World Champion, Gilera's Umberto Masetti.

After this success, Count Agusta believed that the following year, 1953, would see his much-improved machines dominate their respective classes. After Les Graham had taken one of the singles to victory in the 125 cc TT, everyone thought that this confidence was well founded. However, 'Lady Luck' was to dash these hopes when, at the beginning of the second lap in the Senior TT, Les Graham crashed at the bottom of Bray Hill and was fatally injured.

Following Graham's death, the other MV riders could not tame the 500 four that year, although Bandirola did finish second in the final round in Spain. Count Agusta had also signed Carlo Ubbiali from rival FB Mondial, but although he won the 125 cc race in the German GP, at Schotten, the title went to NSU.

It was also at Schotten that Carlo Bandirola gave the new 349.3 cc (47.5 × 49.3 mm) four its first victory, after Graham had débuted the machine in the Junior TT. Unfortunately, the FIM announced that the result would not count towards the Championship, as several of the leading riders had refused to compete in the interests of safety.

MV gave a number of riders 'one-off' race tests that year, in an attempt to find a suitable replacement for the sorely-missed Les Graham. These included the Englishman Bill Lomas and the German Hans Peter Müller.

For the 1954 season, Count Agusta signed Lomas, together with Dickie Dale. They joined Bandirola and the former Gilera rider Nello Pagani. In the 125 cc category, Sandford, and Ubbiali were the mainstream riders, while MV tried a number of others at different races throughout the season, including Copeta, Lottes, Genevini, Bertoni, Columbo and Sala, the last rider providing victory at Monza. Dale rode an extremely competent race to win the final 500 cc GP of the year, in Spain, in October. Generally, however, 1954 was to prove a poor season for MV. With NSU dominating the Lightweight categories, Moto Guzzi the 350 cc class and Gilera the 'Blue Riband' 500 cc division.

This prompted the Count to take action, and at last he gained the services of the Norton star Ray

Right
The 1957 IoM 125 cc TT, which was run over the Clypse circuit. Carlo Ubbiali (25) has just overtaken Sammy Miller (Mondial) at Governor's Bridge. Ubbiali finished second, Miller sixth

Below
Privateer Bill Webster (Earles/MV, 149) and Len Cooper (Purslow/Triumph) chat with the Mayor of Scarborough before the start of the 150 cc race, 14 July 1958. Webster was a close friend of Count Agusta and acted as a 'talent scout' for the Gallarate factory

Amm, who was to ride for the team in 1955. At the same time, both Dale and Lomas left to ride for Moto Guzzi. Other new signings for the Gallarate team were Umberto Masetti, Tito Forconi, Luigi Taveri and Remo Venturi. With Bandirola, Pagani, Copeta and Ubbiali, MV started the 1955 season with a total of *nine* riders.

With NSU in retirement, the appearance of a brand-new 203 cc (68 × 56 mm) dohc single for the 250 cc GP class, a 175 cc (63 × 56 mm) version for the Italian Formula 2 events, and improvements to the four-cylinder models, MV appeared well-organized for a major offensive. However, events were to conspire against the company's hopes.

First, Ray Amm was killed during his début race, while riding a 350 four at Imola on Easter Monday. This was a major blow, since Count Agusta had seen Amm as very much the successor to Les Graham and leader of the MV team. Then, although contracted to Moto Guzzi in the larger classes, Bill Lomas still managed somehow to get the best of both worlds by being entered by MV on one of the new 203 cc singles—he would have won the Championship too,

Below

The fabulous 500 six-cylinder model. It was only raced once by John Hartle, for it was no longer needed after both Gilera and Guzzi quit at the end of 1957

Above
Carlo Ubbiali won a total of nine world titles, eight of them on MV Agusta machinery. He retired at the end of 1960 to concentrate on the family business

influence, and somehow he managed to make a valuable contribution to the team's efforts over the following few years, without coming into conflict with the autocratic Count.

The big news for 1956 was the arrival of the young English rider John Surtees, who had signed to race MV machinery in October of the previous year. He was to ride in both 350 and 500 cc classes. Backing him up in the larger classes would be Masetti, Bandirola and Forconi, while Taveri, Ubbiali and Venturi would ride in the 125 and 250 cc events.

The 203 cc single was shelved in favour of a larger 248.2 cc (72.6 × 60 mm) model, although it had been hoped that a new twin would be ready (in fact, this was not to be raced regularly until the 1959 season). A similar situation transpired in the 350 cc class, where Count Agusta announced that a new 348.8 cc (62 × 57.8 mm) twin would probably compete in place of the smaller four. In the event, however, this was never to leave the prototype stage. The 125

Below
Carlo Ubbiali (36) leads his MV team-mate, Tarquinio Provini, at the Manx Arms, Onchan, during the 1959 125 cc TT. Provini went on to win the race after Ubbiali was slowed by a sick motor

except that he was denied victory in the Dutch TT after a refuelling incident (his 'crime' was that he had not stopped his engine while receiving petrol!). MV took some consolation in the fact that Ubbiali gained the 125 cc title, with Taveri second and Venturi third.

On the technical front, a major improvement on the 500 four was the adoption of new telescopic front forks, in which the wheel spindle was carried in lugs forward of the fork axis. Multi-rate coil springs, operating above the light-alloy sliders, were left exposed. New large-diameter duplex brakes were built into the front wheel. Each was of the single-leading-shoe type. The new front end greatly improved the previous border-line handling, while the new front anchor gave significantly increased stopping power.

Another important development, but this time in the organization, was the appointment of former rider Nello Pagani as team manager, although it is true to say that Count Agusta's hand remained firmly on the tiller. However, Pagani did have some single and 500 four continued much as before, but with detail improvements.

The addition of John Surtees to the Gallarate team marked a turning point in its history. Not only was he a brilliant rider, but also a capable engineer with the knack of pinpointing faults on a machine; something which no other rider, except Les Graham, had been able to do for the MV engineers.

It must also be said that Surtees arrived just as the 500 four was reaching a level where its speed was becoming matched by its reliability, while it was blessed with acceptable handling and roadholding qualities.

Each year the machine had been consistently improved in detail, and was giving nearly 70 bhp at 10,500 rpm, pushing its maximum speed on the very fastest circuits to the 155 mph mark. For 1956 the frame was lower than before, providing superior penetration, which was exploited to the full by a new, comprehensive, streamlined 'dustbin' shell at the front (at that time only used for events such as the Belgian and Italian GPs; for the TT and Ulster, only a small handlebar fairing was fitted).

In the 1956 500 cc world title series, Surtees and MV were greatly assisted by the fact that their main rival, Gilera, was without Geoff Duke and Reg

Above
Works mechanic Arturo Magni making adjustments to John Surtees' 1960 Senior TT mount. John's father, Jack, looks on

Overleaf
Surtees on his way to yet another victory during the 1960 500 cc German GP at Solitude. He averaged 92.7 mph for the 18-lap, 127.7-mile race

Armstrong. Both had been suspended for six months, due to the support they had given to the private riders who went on strike at the Dutch TT in the previous year. This allowed John to build up a considerable lead in the Championship by winning both the Senior TT and the 500 cc Dutch TT.

The first Surtees-Duke clash, on their respective four-cylinder 'fire engines', came at the Belgian GP—the fastest event on the calendar. Over the famous 8.8-mile Spa Francorchamps course, in the heart of the Ardennes, Duke rocketed ahead and, in

Rhodesian Gary Hocking with his 'private' 250 MV twin at the Spanish Grand Prix, April 1961. He rode superbly to defeat the entire Honda team mounted on the latest four-cylinder models

the process, shattered the outright lap record. Then on lap 13, when leading by nearly a minute, his Gilera expired with piston trouble.

After this, Surtees was left to win at his own pace, his third victory, in a row, effectively meaning that he could not be beaten in the Championship. This result was to stand him in good stead, as in the very next round, at Solitude, in West Germany, he crashed in the 350 cc race and broke his arm, sidelining himself for the rest of the season. Even so, with the season only half over, he had amassed enough points to secure the 1956 500 cc World Championship. However, the Solitude accident ruined any chances of scoring a double on the smaller four-cylinder model.

In the Lightweight classes, Ubbiali displayed his mastery by winning five of the six races in both the 125 cc and 250 cc classes, becoming double World Champion.

Count Agusta had witnessed his best year, MV gaining three of the four solo titles and countless wins and lap records in the process. The year had also been one of intense technical development. For example, the factory had *three* types of 350 cc machine on the stocks at the time: a four, a twin and a single. It was also experimenting with both fuel injection and desmodromic (positive) valve operation. Yet another project was a 125 cc double-knocker single with a box-section, light-alloy, *riveted* frame. The top portion of this frame served as a fuel and oil container, while the engine-gearbox unit completed the frame at the bottom.

However, perhaps the most interesting project of all was a top secret 499.2 cc (48×46 mm) six-cylinder model. It was not revealed to the public until several months later, during practice for the 1957 Italian GP. The six-cylinder 500 was only raced once—at Monza, in September 1958, when John Hartle retired after a big scrap with Dickie Dale on a works BMW. Hartle revealed later: 'It buzzed to 10,800 rpm—only 300 revs more than the four—but it had a very narrow power-band and lacked torque. It had six carburettors and could have done with six or more gears instead of five.' These reasons, combined with the withdrawal of the Mondial, Guzzi and Gilera factories at the end of 1957, were probably why it did not ultimately replace the four.

In fact, 1957 was a poor year for MV, Mondial taking both the Lightweight titles, Guzzi the 350 cc class and Gilera the 500 cc. However, without these three rivals, MV made a clean sweep of the 1958 series, Ubbiali becoming the 125 cc Champion, Provini (a new signing that year) taking the 250 cc title, and Surtees a double Champion in the 350/500 cc categories. The only competition came in the smallest class, where the desmodromic Ducati singles made a strong challenge, winning three of the seven rounds.

The long-serving Carlo Bandirola announced his retirement at the end of the year, after finally taking the 500 cc Italian Senior Championship title. John Hartle had been signed for the 1958 season as back-up to Surtees, replacing another Englishman, Terry Shepherd, who had carried out this task in 1957, although a hand injury, sustained at the TT, meant that he only contested three rounds. The three-year period embracing 1958, 1959 and 1960 saw MV unbeaten in its quest for solo world titles, with

Ubbiali and Surtees taking the lion's share of the honours between them.

Provini left to join Morini at the end of 1959, his replacement being the young Rhodesian Gary Hocking. He was 'promoted' by Count Agusta to lead the team after both Ubbiali and Surtees finally hung up their leathers at the end of 1960.

The only 'new' machine during this era was the long-awaited 247 cc (53 × 56 mm) twin, which had finally been introduced for the 1959 season. Producing 36 bhp at 12,000 rpm, it had a maximum speed of 137 mph and weighed 109 kg (238 lb).

In fact, the twin had been ready for a number of years, and even raced on a few occasions, on one of which it gained victory in the 1957 Belgian Grand Prix. Technically, it consisted of a pair of 125, dohc, single-cylinder top-ends mated to a common crankcase with a six-speed gearbox. Because of this, and its long gestation period, the machine proved very reliable in service. The only real problem came from the rivalry between team-mates Ubbiali and Provini, who both wanted to win. This did not just extend

Hocking at speed with the 500 MV four, on his way to winning the Race of the Year at Mallory Park, September 1961

to the World Championship series, but to Italian races too. The rivalry led to a number of controversies during the 1959 season, and it was only resolved when Provini quit MV at the end of that year to join Morini.

Other team news included Hartle's announcement that he was returning to the ranks of the privateers with a brace of Nortons in April 1960, and that the former Morini rider Emilio Mendogni had signed for MV as a replacement. He would join Surtees, Venturi, Hocking and Ubbiali.

A few weeks later, it transpired that Hartle was to be loaned a pair of works MV fours for the IoM TT; he responded by winning the Junior and coming second in the Senior. Then it was back to his own single-cylinder Nortons for the remainder of the season, during which he gained victory over his former team-mate, Surtees, at the Ulster in August.

For 1961 Count Agusta cut back MV's racing activities, leaving only one rider, Gary Hocking. He declared that the factory was no longer officially competing and that Hocking would be provided with one factory mechanic and loaned a 250 twin, together with 350 and 500 cc fours. All of these had large 'Privat-MV' logos on their fuel tanks.

In the 250 cc class, Hocking got off to a winning

Mike Hailwood, seen here after the 1961 TT presentations with his father Stan, teamed up with Gary Hocking to form a dynamic duo for the 1962 season on factory MVs. Sadly, it did not last, as after Tom Phillis was killed in June 1962, Hocking quit bikes for cars, but then suffered a fatal crash himself

start over the tortuous Montjuich Park circuit in Barcelona, the home of that year's Spanish GP. However, after this early success, the lone MV twin was simply blown into the weeds by a swarm of Japanese Honda fours at the next two rounds in West Germany and France. This was more than Count Agusta could stand, and the twin was promptly retired. Hocking made no such mistakes in the larger classes, taking both titles, although the fours suffered more than their usual mechanical problems that year due to the 'Privat' farce.

After some excellent showings on his single-cylinder AJS and Norton machinery, Mike Hailwood

was provided with a brace of MV fours for the Italian and Finnish rounds at the end of the season. He did well enough (including a 500 cc victory at Monza) to convince Count Agusta that he should be allowed to join Hocking as a full member of the team in the following year.

The 1962 classic season got under way with tremendous duels between the two MV men in the Junior and Senior TTs—they were allowed to ride as they wished, without 'team' orders. The result was that Hailwood won the Junior and Hocking the Senior, the latter with a record lap at 105.75 mph.

The Rhodesian then announced his retirement from motorcycle racing, citing the fatal accident that occurred to his friend Tom Phillis, while riding a 285 cc Honda four in the Junior TT, as the reason. This left Mike Hailwood as the lone MV rider, but he did not have things all his own way as, by now, Honda was making a serious challenge in the 350 cc class. Soon, a full-sized 350 cc four-cylinder machine was introduced to replace the 285 cc model used by Phillis and Jim Redman in the TT. Flown to Europe, this proved so superior to the ageing Italian machine that Redman outsped Hailwood with ease in the remaining classics, finishing the year as World Champion. Once again, Count Agusta decided to retire from the class rather than fight. This left only the 500 cc class, in which Hailwood took the title in 1963, 1964 and 1965.

In that last year, an entirely new combination made its entry into the Grand Prix arena—Giacomo Agostini and the 350 MV *three-cylinder* model. This was just the tonic Count Agusta needed, as his dream had always been for an Italian to win in the larger classes aboard one of his bikes. 'Ago' had made his name racing for the tiny Morini factory in the 250 Senior Italian Championship, in which he had convincingly beaten the pairing of Provini and the four-cylinder Benelli in 1964. Thus, the Count had signed Agostini for 1965—and, at last, released the three-cylinder design which had been conceived as early as 1958.

The 343.9 cc (52 × 54 mm), across-the-frame triple had its cylinders inclined forward some 10 degrees from the vertical. Other items of technical interest included three 28 mm Dell'Orto carburettors, a seven-speed gearbox, 18 in. wheels, a 16-litre (3.5-gallon) fuel tank, and a four-cam, 240 mm drum front brake of immense size and power. With 62.5 bhp at 13,500 rpm on tap, the new MV could reach 150 mph. Not only was it almost as fast as the 500 four, but its handling and roadholding were definite improvements!

Above

The 497.5 cc (53 × 56.4 mm) MV Agusta 'fire engine', as used by Surtees, Hartle, Hocking and Hailwood, among others

Below

Daytona, February 1964: Mike Hailwood gets the 'okay' from father Stan during a high-speed session, in which he set a new one-hour record at 144.22 mph on the 500 MV

Above
Hailwood bumps the four-cylinder MV into life at the start of his winning ride in the 1965 Senior TT

Right
The first appearance of the experimental, Peter Durr-designed 125 MV two-stroke during practice at Cesenatico, May 1965. The project was soon abandoned

Agostini and the MV three made a sensational Grand Prix début, when they won the 350 cc race of a very wet West German GP at the Nürburgring in April 1965. Honda team captain and multi-World Champion Jim Redman had crashed in a vain attempt to match the flying Italian duo. Moreover, Agostini would have won the 350 cc world title that year had not a broken contact-breaker spring robbed him of victory in the final round in Japan when leading by a huge margin.

Although Hailwood retained his 500 cc crown that year, he was clearly upset by the amount of attention his Italian team-mate was receiving. Thus when Honda made him an offer of big money to race for them in 1966, he accepted.

Another development in 1965, but this time a distinct failure, had been an all-new MV two-stroke for the 125 cc class. Powered by a 124.5 cc (54.2 × 54 mm) horizontal single, with disc-valve induction, it was soon shelved through a mixture of poor reliability and lack of performance. The engine was the work of the German two-stroke specialist Peter Durr, and its rider none other than Walter Villa, later a four-times World Champion on Harley-Davidson (Aermacchi) two-stroke twins in the 1970s.

Throughout 1966 Agostini and Hailwood had some tremendous battles, the Honda rider winning the 350 cc title and Agostini taking the 500 cc honours. MV's success came with an enlarged three, rather than an updated four-cylinder model. At first, the capacity was increased to 377 cc, then 420 cc and, finally, 497.9 cc (62 × 55.3 mm), although the last did not appear until 1967.

Hailwood and Agostini duplicated their championship results in 1967. However, the MV rider's

Count Agusta signed the former Morini rider Giacomo Agostini for 1965. During his first ride at Modena, in March that year, the newcomer blotted his copy-book by dropping the 500 MV. However, he recovered to become the most successful rider of all time, with a record 15 world titles and 123 Grand Prix victories

success only came after a bitter struggle with Hailwood, each of them winning five of the ten Grands Prix contested. An extra second place made all the difference to Agostini. At Monza, the 500 cc race should have brought Hailwood the title, but, when two laps from the finish and with a half-lap lead over the Italian, his Honda's gearbox refused to function.

Hailwood's retirement and Honda's withdrawal from the sport made Agostini's task much easier in 1968. He won all 17 championship races he contested that year.

He repeated his double 350/500 cc title act over the next three years: 1969, 1970 and 1971. Usually, 'Ago' was the sole MV rider in the classics during this period, except for a brief spell when Angelo Bergamonti was signed in the latter part of the 1970 season. Bergamonti, formerly with Aermacchi, actually won the 1970 500 cc Spanish GP after Agostini

Left
Giacomo Agostini—good looks and great riding skill

Below
Angelo Bergamonti, back-up rider to 'Ago', scored only one Grand Prix victory for MV—the 1970 Spanish on the 350 three-cylinder model

was forced to retire, but he was killed before the GP season had even got under way during an Italian national meeting at Riccione in early 1971.

Earlier, in March 1969, a new six-cylinder racer had been tested by Agostini at Modena. This had been developed in response to Honda's similar model, but the Japanese firm's withdrawal meant that it was never used in anger. Its 348.8 cc (43.3 × 39.5 mm) engine revved to 16,000 rpm and produced a claimed 72 bhp. A 500 cc version was also on the drawing board. This was a totally new bike and not an update of the 1950s design.

February 1971 was a decisive date in the MV racing story, because it was then that Count Domenico Agusta suffered a fatal heart attack while in Milan at a business meeting. For some 25 years, Domenico Agusta had controlled his industrial enterprise with a fist of iron, yet, at the same time, had authorized the expenditure of a vast fortune on the racing effort. For, despite the fact that he seldom went to see his bikes in action, it was the Count's untiring personal enthusiasm which had been behind the company's successful track exploits. He, and he alone, decided the racing policy, how much money would be spent on it, and where the riders would compete. Why he went racing at all remains largely

Agostini's 500 MV three at the 1971 Italian GP

Overleaf
Czech GP at Brno, 1973: Giacomo Agostini (shown here) and Phil Read made it an MV 1-2, the Italian getting the verdict. The championship title, however, finally went to the Englishman

a mystery. Initially, it had been to publicize his production motorcycles, but in later years it could only have been his pride and constant craving for success which had driven him on.

After Domenico's death, the sole survivor of the four Agusta brothers, Corrado, took over as boss of the company. By that time, it was the largest helicopter company in Italy and a major player on the world aviation scene. Many pundits forecast the imminent demise of MV in racing, but this did not happen until several years later. Agostini remained with the company (although several pressmen had linked him with Benelli) to score yet another double championship in 1971.

Things were not so easy in 1972, however, and the MV rider struggled against the 'Flying Finn' Jarno Saarinen in the 350 cc class. Nello Pagani's

Above
Phil Read on the MV (1) on his way to victory in the 1974 500 cc Finnish GP at Imatra. The other rider is Suzuki-mounted Barry Sheene

Above right
Read in winning form at Cadwell Park with his 500 MV, 22 September 1974

Right
MV's last GP victory came at the 1976 West German GP. Here Agostini, on the lone Italian four-cylinder machine, streaks away at the start of the race to herald the end of an era

son, Alberto, teamed with 'Ago', winning the 500 cc Yugoslav GP in the process.

In 1973 Agostini took the 350 cc Championship, his 30th and last for the Gallarate marque. The Englishman Phil Read had joined the team and carried off the coveted 500 cc title. However, things might have been very different for the MV men had Saarinen not been killed in an accident at Monza, during the fourth round of the series.

As for machinery, MV had introduced a brand-new, 349.8 cc (53 × 38.2 mm), ultra-short-stroke

four-cylinder model. This had débuted at the 1971 Italian GP. Then, as with the three, a larger-capacity 433 cc (56 × 44 mm) version had appeared in 1973, followed later that year by a full-size 498.6 cc (58 × 47 mm) model.

For 1974 the larger engine had been redesigned with revised 57 × 49.4 mm (499.5 cc) bore and stroke dimensions. Agostini left to join Yamaha that year, Phil Read being joined by Gianfranco Bonera. The MVs only competed in the larger class, the English rider winning the title, while Bonera was runner-up in his first year of Grand Prix competition.

From then on, it was largely downhill all the way, with the two-stroke challenge, led by Yamaha and Suzuki, in full swing and Yamaha's man Agostini becoming the new 500 cc Champion in 1975. MV won only two GPs—the Belgian (for the 18th time in 18 years!) and the final round at Brno, in Czechoslovakia.

On the technical front, MV tried everything to counter the 'strokers', but to no avail. Modifications included new chassis with both conventional twin shocks and single-shock cantilever rear suspension, triple disc brakes and even a wing-shaped aerofoil.

In the following year, 1976, MV quit competition on an official basis. However, in a very peculiar set of circumstances, Agostini returned to ride 'privately-entered' MVs, backed by the Italian oil company Api. Although the works was not supposed to be taking a direct interest, there was still a full team of factory mechanics and a *new* 350 four.

The new machine was very quick, but it was also exceptionally unreliable, at least in the beginning. On the odd occasion when it did keep going, however, it was a potential race winner, as demonstrated when 'Ago' took it to victory in the Dutch TT at Assen. MV Agusta's last classic victory came at the final Grand Prix of 1976, in the 500 cc class at the Nürburgring, West Germany.

Except for 'demonstration' appearances, including ones by Agostini (Brands Hatch) and Read (Cadwell Park), this really was the end. The accountants who controlled the Agusta group's purse strings had the final say, leaving enthusiasts the world over with only their memories. The fabulous racing machines which had given MV a record number of championship and race wins were placed under lock and key at the Gallarate factory complex.

Today, some of those machines have found their way into private collections. Others reside in the factory's own museum in Gallarate, as a lasting reminder of the fantastic achievements gained by the most successful motorcycle racing team of the post-World War 2 period.

11
Parilla

Giovanni Parrilla (note the two 'r's, one of which was dropped in the interests of easier pronunciation when used as the marque name) was born in the South of Italy during 1912, after the Parrilla family had emigrated from Barcelona, Spain. When he was three years old, the family moved yet again, this time to Mantova in the North of Italy. Eventually, they moved once more to Milan when Giovanni was a teenager.

Giovanni's first business enterprise was based in Via Sabotino on the outskirts of Milan where, from a small garage-cum-workshop, he offered a repair service for diesel injection pumps and acted as a wholesaler for Bosch sparking plugs. His move to the ranks of motorcycle manufacturers began shortly after the war when, in 1946, he set out to design and build his own racing machine. When this subsequently made its début at Lecco, in the hands of Nino Grieco, on 1 October 1946, it could claim

The 1949 Parilla 250 Bialbero *(twin-cam) racer. It was one of the very first completely-new racing designs to emerge from Italy in the post-war era*

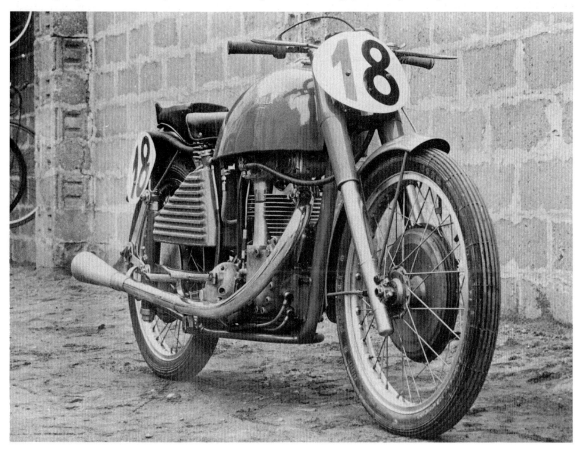

Bare castings for Parilla 250 cc single-overhead-cam racing engine, 1948

to have been the first all-new Italian racing design since the cessation of hostilities.

In many ways, the new bike displayed Parrilla's enthusiasm for British motorcycles, which had endured since his youth. Later, he was to admit that his favourite was the camshaft Norton.

The newcomer had not been designed by Parrilla himself, but by the gifted engineer Ing. Guiseppe Salmaggi, who had been responsible for the Gilera Saturno just before the outbreak of war in 1939.

Salmaggi's instruction from his employer was that the machine was to look like a Norton, with a single vertical cylinder and bevel-driven overhead camshaft—Giovanni Parrilla was of the opinion that a machine appearing British in design would sell well on the Italian market. In fact, there were two proto-type machines. Both were 246.32 cc (66 × 72 mm) singles, having a single overhead camshaft driven

by straight-cut bevel gears connected by a split shaft with an Oldhams coupling. There was a series of gears within the timing case, and yet more for the primary drive—not a chain in sight!

Although it might not have appeared so to the casual observer, the crankcase casting embraced the four-speed, close-ratio gearbox and also the clutch and primary drive, providing full unit construction. Because of the poor quality fuel available at the time, Salmaggi was forced to use the low compression ratio of 6:1. This meant that power output was severely restricted—actually around 15 bhp at 6200 rpm.

Both prototypes sported a fully-welded, loop-type frame with a single front downtube. Plunger rear suspension with adjustable friction dampers ultimately gave way to a swinging-arm arrangement at the rear, while the original girder front forks were changed to leading-axle telescopics.

Dry-sump lubrication meant that the castor-based oil was carried in a large-capacity, heavily-finned tank located beneath the saddle.

Production of the Corsa (racer), together with a roadgoing sportster, began in 1947. Both were displayed at the Milan show that year, where they aroused considerable interest.

The Corsa featured truly massive 260 mm (10.25 in.) aluminium brake drums at both front and rear—they were soon nicknamed *padellone* (large frying pan). Power had been increased to 18 bhp, which provided a maximum speed of 92 mph, around 7 mph up on the prototype bikes.

One of the 350 Parillas raced so successfully in Germany during 1950 and 1951 by Hermann Gablenz and Roland Schell. Rider/engineer Schell even produced his own six-speed gearbox for the bike

A 1953 Parilla 250 dohc single with Earles-type front forks, as raced by works rider Nino Grieco

In 1947 work had also begun on a *Bialbero* (double-cam) version. When this made its début in the following year, it pumped out an impressive 21 bhp at 8500 rpm, while maximum speed was a shade over the magic ton.

Like the single-knocker version, the newcomer sported a vertical drive shaft and bevel gears. There was a series of gears operating the inlet and exhaust camshafts by means of pinions. Each cam was carried by a roller race at the drive end, and a ball race at the other end. The cams activated the valves through flat-top tappets; valve springs were of the hairpin variety and were exposed. The separate dohc drive box sat atop the cylinder head in much the same way as the double-knocker Manx Norton.

Both the cylinder head and barrel were in light alloy, the latter being sleeved with a reborable liner. Once again, at 7:8:1, the compression ratio was on the low side, although the forged Borgo three-ring piston was provided with a massive dome. The special steel connecting rod was double-webbed at top and bottom for additional strength, while the caged-roller big-end was of generous dimensions.

In an attempt to prune weight (the single-knocker bikes being on the heavy side), Ing. Salmaggi provided the *Bialbero* with as many engine castings in electron alloy as possible—including the crankcase assembly. This had the effect of reducing dry weight to a more manageable 115 kg (250 lb).

One notable feature of the double-cam 250 was its flexibility which, for a racing unit, was truly outstanding. The power came in at an engine speed as low as 3500 rpm. Some of this could well have been due to the fact that the company preferred to carry out its tests on the road, rather than on the engine test-bench. Thus, rider input occurred at an early stage in the development programme.

In 1950 the 250 was joined by a 350 cc version. Its début came in March that year, at Marseilles, in the capable hands of Nello Pagani. This first outing was marred when a camshaft drive sheared.

One of the new 350s, together with a similar 250 cc double-knocker, was sent to Germany to be ridden by Hermann Gablenz and Roland Schell (later to win fame on Horex machinery). Over the next couple of years, the pair dominated a large part of the German racing scene, the larger model proving extremely competitive against the likes of DKW and AJS machinery. Working in co-operation with the Parilla factory, Schell, a talented engineer in his own right, developed a six-speed gearbox which was fitted to at least one of the machines.

Other notable successes gained by the *Bialbero* Parillas included Piero Cavaciuti's 250 cc class victory in the 1950 Milano-Taranto, and some excellent showings in the classics by long-serving works rider, Nino Grieco. The latter gained sixth and fifth places in the 1951 and 1952 Swiss GPs respectively (on the 250 cc model).

During 1952 factory boss, Giovanni Parrilla, realized that the days of the bevel-driven 250 and 350 double-knockers were rapidly coming to an end. At the Milan show towards the end of the year, the first *Camme Rialzata* (high-cam) was shown. This was the 175 Fox roadster, and although a racing version was still some way off, it did at least point the way forward for the Milanese marque.

A prototype chain-driven dohc 125 single appeared during practice for the 1952 Italian GP at Monza, but it did not start in the race—or, for that matter, receive any further development. However, another version (still with chain drive) was built and tested during 1953 and 1954.

Parilla had intended the 125 to be a serious GP contender, but in the end it was allowed to fade quietly from the scene. Other prototypes, including a new 250, came and went, but none achieved any lasting success. Instead, Parilla switched its efforts into producing an over-the-counter production racer. The first of these, the 175 Competizione, was available during 1953 and 1954. For 1955 the Competizione was modified and replaced with the 175 MSDS, the most notable difference being the replace-

Above

Experimental 175 double-knocker Parilla, on display at the 1955 Milan Show

Above right

Gianfranco Muscio before the start of what was probably a short-circuit Italian class event in 1958 or 1959; it was not the Giro d'Italia because of the huge rear sprocket. The engine is the final development of the 250 cc Bialbero mounted in a late frame with Amadoro brakes

Right

This Parilla 125 cc (54 × 54 mm), disc-valve, horizontal single made its début in 1960. It developed 23 bhp at 11,500 rpm

ment of the Earles-type front forks with conventional telescopics. Later, 200 and 250 cc versions were built, but only for the North American market.

In fact, the high-cam Parilla was only really successful in Stateside events where, during the early 1960s, the 250 model was often *the* bike to beat. This

*Parilla 125 cc two-stroke racing engine, April 1960.
Although showing considerable potential, it was not
raced until several years later, when it was
campaigned by the former Morini rider Gianpiero
Zubani in the 1965 Italian Senior Championship series*

was due, in no small part, to the performances of
Norris Rancourt on the Orrin Hall machine. Rancourt
chalked up a stack of wins and places from 1962
through to 1965, by which time the Yamaha TD1
twin was becoming all-dominant. Ron Grant also
rode the Orrin Hall-tuned Parilla to annex runner-up
spot in the 1964 US Grand Prix, held at Daytona.

Amazingly, Hall's bike used the basic production
Parilla high-cam engine with its 'square' 68 mm bore
and stroke dimensions. He insisted that the success
was not due to any special parts, but rather: 'Very
minor modifications and extremely precise assembly. All I've done is spend lots of time, and everything is strictly production Parilla items available to
anyone.'

The only other racing Parilla of any note was a
horizontal, single-cylinder two-stroke, which made
its début in early 1960, but was not completely
developed until 1965. Ridden by Gianpiero Zubani

in the Italian Senior Championship series that year,
it had first been announced in November 1959 and
was the work of Ing. Piero Bossaglia.

The reason why this project took so long to come
to fruition was that Giovanni Parrilla had sold out
to a holding company in 1962, and the horizontal
'stroker' was very much his baby. When the new
owners of the Parilla factory showed no particular
interest in racing, Signor Parrilla decided to take
over the project himself.

The machine had disc-valve induction and, in its
1965 form, developed 23 bhp at the rear wheel. Bore
and stroke were 54 × 54 mm, and peak power was
developed at 11,500 rpm. The gearbox was a five-
speeder, but Giovanni Parrilla had renewed his
alliance with Ing. Salmaggi, who designed an eight-
speed cluster.

Unfortunately, this, and a proposed 125 cc twin
for Grand Prix events, failed to be developed further. Instead, Giovanni Parrilla and his son switched
to a successful line of go-kart engines, while the original Moto Parilla motorcycle company finally closed
its doors in 1967. It had become a victim of the
recession which had swept through the Italian two-
wheel industry in the mid 1960s.

Index